Wild Edible Plants of Colorado

Lincoln Town Press

I0109432

Copyright © 2020, 2022, 2025 by Charles W. Kane
First edition, Forth printing

Library of Congress Control Number: 2020942123
ISBN 10: 0998287199 and ISBN 13: 9780998287195

    Wild Edible Plants of Colorado is intended solely for educational purposes. The publisher and author disclaim any liability arising from the use of any plant listed in this book.

Printed on 100% recycled paper

Introduction	2	Heartleaf Bittercress	23	Salsify	43
Amaranth	4	Indian Rice Grass	24	Serviceberry	44
Asparagus	5	Lambsquarters	25	Sheep's Sorrel	45
Beeplant	6	Lemonade Berry	26	Smartweed	46
Bilberry	7	Mallow	27	Spiderwort	47
Box Elder	8	Mariposa Lily	28	Squaw Apple	48
Bracken Fern	9	Marsh Marigold	29	Thimbleberry	49
Buffalo Gourd	10	Monkey Flower	30	Thistle	50
Cattail	11	Mountain Parsley	31	Tuber Starwort	51
Checkermallow	12	Mullein	32	Tule	52
Chokecherry	13	Nettle	33	Tumble Mustard	53
Creeping Hollygrape	14	Orach	34	Watercress	54
Currant	15	Ox–Eye Daisy	35	Wild Onion	55
Evening Primrose	16	Panicgrass	36	Wild Rose	56
Fairybells	17	Pinyon Pine	37	Wild Strawberry	57
Gambel Oak	18	Plantain	38	Wild Sunflower	58
Gooseberry	19	Prickly Pear	39	Wintercress	59
Greenthread	20	Purslane	40	Yellowdock	60
Ground Cherry	21	Raspberry	41	Yucca	61
Hawthorn	22	Russian Olive	42	Index	62

Introduction

Colorado's Wild Edible Flora

To understand Colorado's plant life, it's important to first glimpse the state's topography and weather patterns. Succinctly, the state is a merger of high mountains (Southern Rocky Mountains), plains/grassland (40% of the state to the east), and western arid basin, range, and plateau. The region's weather patterns are as equally diverse. Much of the rain/snowfall that occurs in the mountains is due to elevation (higher elevation equals more precipitation). Pikes Peak, a notorious 'thunderstorm generator', is one example of this weather-mountain interplay. The Plains are associated with an entirely different weather pattern; most precipitation occurs as rainfall during the growing season. Summertime afternoon thunderstorms are common. Western/Southwestern Colorado is lower, warmer, and drier than the central mountain region. Providing a necessary plant-life boost, weak monsoonal rainfall occurs during the summer.

Colorado maintains more xerophytic plant life to the west, alpine/subalpine plants in the middle, and prairie plants to the east. It's difficult to correlate types of edible plants with the state's various zones; however, as a non-scientific, off-the-cuff observation, it seems that there are more Mustards and annual greens in western parts than elsewhere. Berry providers (mostly Rose family) dominate the Rockies, and as for the Plains, grains (grass seed) and roots/tubers/bulbs tend to be more abundant.

What is a Wild Edible Plant?

A wild edible should be considered more than simply a plant (or plant part) that can be chewed and swallow without harm or benefit (in other words, a 'neutral' plant). Nor is it one that is medicinal (high in physiologically-influencing compounds). It certainly is not a poisonous plant (very high in these compounds). A true wild edible plant is one that contains calories (and nutrients), but very few to no physiologically-influencing compounds, or through mild processing can made safe.

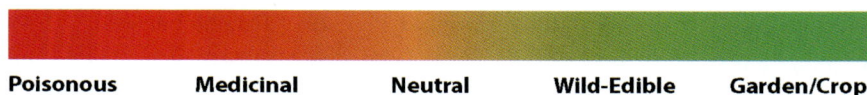

| Poisonous | Medicinal | Neutral | Wild-Edible | Garden/Crop |

Environmental Concerns & Legalities

None of the plants listed are threatened or endangered. In fact, many of them are considered 'weeds'. If a species is encountered in a less–than–ideal situation, this mainly due to environmental stress or edge–of–range habitat, it may be worth considering letting the group go undisturbed.

Is plant collection on public land legal? It's complicated. Technically, it's mostly illegal. However, if engaged in respectfully and sensibly, it's like driving 1 mph over the speed limit...there's no harm done, of consequence. Take heed though, describing this point to a nosy marplot and the ticket–happy forest ranger in their employ may be a hard sell.

Proper Identification

It's a wise idea to know without a doubt what is being consumed prior to its consumption. Besides this publication, I recommend the use of a field guide (or two) to confirm species identification. Most of the time, cases of mistaken identity will not cause serious harm. However, mistakes with Carrot, Lily, and Nightshade family plants may be deadly.

Resources & Acknowledgments

For supportive classification/distribution information, I referred to the SEINet database, Flora of North America (via efloras.org), and Biota of North America Program site.

Creative Commons/Public Domain photos include the following: 'Bilberries (Vaccinium myrtillus) in Kerava, Finland' by Anneli Salo, CC BY–SA 3.0 (p7–bottom photo). 'Panicum capillare sl25' by Stefan Lefnaer. CC BY-SA 4.0 (p36-circle photo).

Poisonous Plants

The following are a small number of problematic genera found in Colorado. This is by no means a complete list.

Locoweed (Astragalus)

Water hemlock (Cicuta)

Water hemlock (Cicuta)

Poison hemlock (Conium)

Poison hemlock (Conium)

Peavine (Lathyrus)

Horse nettle (Solanum)

False hellebore (Veratrum)

Deathcamas (Anticlea)

Amaranth
Amaranthus spp.

Other Common Names
Tumbleweed amaranth, Powell's amaranth, Prostrate pigweed, Sand amaranth, Carelessweed, Quelites

Range & Habitat
Colorado is home to 9 species of Amaranthus, though only 4–5 are abundant. Of this bunch, all are small to medium–sized upright weeds; except for Prostrate pigweed (tends to be ground–hugging) and Tumbleweed pigweed (yes...looks like Tumbleweed). They are common to disturbed soils such as old fields, ditches, and roadsides. They need full sun and somewhat moist soils to thrive.

Edible Uses
The young leaves of the larger/upright species can be eaten raw (as a forage/salad) early in the season. However, all members are best utilized as a cooked green. A quick boil and freshwater rinse will eliminate some of the plant's oxalate content and make the leaves more palatable so larger quantities can be consumed. Once cooked, the leaves taste much like spinach.

After Amaranth has gone to seed (late summer–fall), strip the dried seed spikes from the top of each plant. Wearing gloves, rub the clusters together to separate the seeds from their spiky encasements. Winnow in a light breeze or fan set on low. The seeds are high in protein and generally nutritious. They can be ground into a meal, cooked like other grains, or soaked and then eaten.

Medicinal Uses, Cautions, & Special Note
There are no significant medicinal uses for Amaranth. Be sure to boil and rinse the leaves if consuming them in larger amounts. This removes some of their oxalate content. Cultivated species were once important Mesoamerican food (seed) crops.

Sustenance Index: High
Pictured: *Amaranthus palmeri*

Asparagus
Asparagus officinalis

Other Common Names
Common asparagus, Garden asparagus, Wild asparagus

Range & Habitat
Asparagus officinalis is a non–native garden/crop cultivar that has escaped its original boundaries and is now found in disturbed and lower–lying/moist soils. A people–plant, it tends not to grows in the wilds, but rather around population centers. Look to field margins, grassy areas, road and trail sides, and untended embankments.

Edible Uses
Clip the emerging spears in the spring. They should be flexible and non–woody. If allowed to grow un–cut the spears develop into the plant's stems and are non–edible.

Steam/sauté/boil 'wild' Aspar-agus spears like the garden–grown/store–bought kind. Seasoned with a little butter and spices they will be equally delicious and nutritious.

Medicinal Uses
The root tea is a traditional European herbal remedy for gout, uric acid–type kidney stones, related joint inflam-mation, and generally overly–acidic urine (imagine a historical cold season western European diet of beef, wheat, and wine/ale).

Cautions & Special Note
Aside from sulfur–smelling urine, there are no cautions for Asparagus consumption.

The spears contain asparagusic acid, which some people after digesting, metabolize into methanethiol, dimethyl sulfide, and other sulfur–based compounds. These are responsible for the Asparagus–smelling urine noticeable after the plant's consumption. Purple cultivars of Asparagus are much higher in antioxidant pigments (anthocyanins) than standard types.

Sustenance Index: Medium
Pictured: *Asparagus officinalis*

Beeplant
Peritoma serrulata (Cleome serrulata)

Other Common Names
Rocky Mountain beeplant, Bee spiderflower

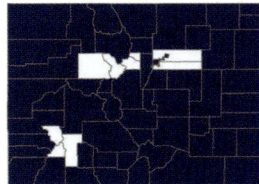

Range & Habitat
Beeplant is a large annual herb of the western mountain states. It's found nearly statewide throughout Colorado. Look for it below the high mountains in disturbed soils: next to dirt roadsides, trailsides, and drainage bottoms/sides. It's a fast grower in response to summertime rains.

Edible Uses
The young leaves, flowers, and pods (green/flexible) are gathered mid–summer. Eat these parts fresh (limited) as a spicy/mustard–like salad addition. Better yet, simmer them for 5–10 minutes and rinse with fresh water. Season to taste and eat solo as a cooked green or add Beeplant to other cooked greens as part of a combo.

   The young pods (seeds still unformed) are pickled like capers, though this will remove much of the pod's natural spiciness. The mature seeds too are edible. They're best soaked, rinsed, dehydrated, ground, and then added in small amounts to other flours.

Medicinal Uses, Cautions, & Special Note
Beeplant is not significantly medicinal, nor are there any cautions for the plant (aside from cautions common to all mustard oil containing plants – see Wintercress). The Pueblo, Navajo, and Apache utilized Beeplant as an edible due to its abundance and non–toxicity. Clammyweed (Polanisia dodecandra), which belongs to the same family (Cleomaceae), grows lower in elevation, but is smaller and has white flowers (with red stamens). It's occasionally listed as edible. Truth be told, it's sticky, poor–tasting, and more fibrous than Beeplant. Edible, but barely. Like Mustard, Beeplant's spiciness is due to its glucosinolate content.

Sustenance Index: Medium
Pictured: *Peritoma serrulata*

6

Bilberry

Vaccinium caespitosum, V. myrtillus, V. scoparium

Other Common Names
Dwarf bilberry, Whortleberry, Grouse whortleberry, Huckleberry

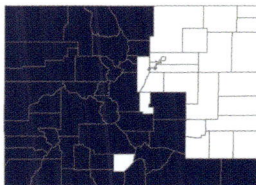

Range & Habitat
Three Vaccinium species are common in Colorado. Although names (Bilberry, Huckleberry, Whortleberry) for each are loosely interchangeable, Bilberry (especially for *Vaccinium myrtillus*) is the best known edible species of the bunch.

Bilberry is found in montane/forested regions throughout the Rockies (and Pacific Northwest). Present at 9000' and above, look for the plant with Aspen, Pine, Fir, Spruce, Doug fir, and/or Gambel oak overhead. Slopes, hillsides, and drainage sides are some of its usual areas.

Edible Uses
Although Blueberry (Vaccinium corymbosum) has a larger fruit, consider Bilberry identical in all edible aspects. A summertime berry, look closely for the fruit hanging beneath the leaves. They are delicious eaten fresh. Additionally, its utility as a dried berry or freshly prepared as a jelly, preserve, or syrup needs little explanation.

As for Bilberry's nutritional value, the fruit contains fair amounts of vitamins A, C, and a number of B vitamins. Potassium, magnesium, and calcium are additionally listed for the fruit.

Medicinal Uses & Cautions
Bilberry fruit extract (Vaccinium myrtillus) has a well–established following as an ocular preventive medicine. It's mostly employed as an antioxidant to slow the progression of cataracts, macular degeneration, and related eye disturbances. Bilberry leaf tea is mildly astringent and traditionally used to counter diarrhea and reduce renal irritation. There are no cautions for Bilberry.

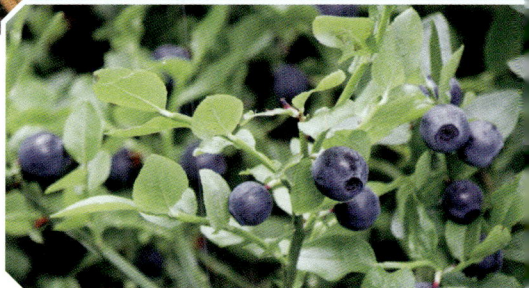

Sustenance Index: Medium
Pictured: *Vaccinium myrtillus*

7

Box Elder
Acer negundo

Other Common Names
Ash–leaf maple

Range & Habitat
A common tree throughout America, look for Box elder at middle elevations (5000'–8000') next to streams and related drainages. In Colorado, this medium–sized tree is not found in the high mountains (Aspen–Fir–Spruce belt), but rather in the lower ranges and foothills. It's intermingled with Cottonwood, Currant, Lemonade berry, and other scrub vegetation. Juniper and Pinyon are additional trees of this zone, however, they are found above Box elder, growing on drier ledges and hillsides.

Edible Uses
A simple trail–forage or pot herb, the very young samaras (winged fruit) are the sought–after item. Eaten as–is the samaras have a not–too coarse texture and neutral taste. They are fine added to salads and/or prepared/seasoned as a cooked green. They are edible for only 1–2 weeks in the spring when immature and greenish–red. Later in the season, they become fibrous and bitter.

Although often cited as an edible part, I find the mature seed to be too bitter for wild food consideration.

Medicinal Uses & Cautions
There are no significant medicinal uses or cautions for Box elder.

Special Note
Box elder is technically a species of Maple (Acer), not Elder (Sambucus) or Ash (Fraxinus). Its parted leaf vaguely resembles an Elder or Ash leaf, hence the common name discombobulation.

Sustenance Index: Low
Pictured: *Acer negundo*

8

Bracken Fern
Pteridium aquilinum

Other Common Names
Bracken, Western bracken fern, Fiddleneck

Range & Habitat
Widespread throughout the Northern Hemisphere, Bracken fern enjoys a significant distribution in Colorado. The fern is common to montane locations, usually with Ponderosa pine. In fact, deep pine needle chuff and dappled shade seem to reliably point to its presence.

Edible Uses
Late spring to early summer Bracken fern begins to sprout anew from its sub–surface rhizomes. When the stem shoots are 8"–1' in height, snip them at ground level using clippers (or hands alone are fine). Cover the shoots with fresh water and add a teaspoon of baking soda and a teaspoon of salt. Boil/simmer the shoots for about 15 minutes. Drain, rinse, add fresh water (with baking soda and salt), and simmer again for another ten minutes. Drain, rinse, season, and serve as an asparagus–like vegetable.

Medicinal Uses & Cautions
There are no medicinal uses for Bracken fern. Livestock poisonings (and animal studies) leave no doubt that this fern is a harbinger of carcinogenic, mutagenic, and neurotoxic principles (mainly, ptaquiloside). There is even a correlation between higher esophageal cancer rates and Japanese whom regularly consume Bracken fern. With that said, it is my opinion that eating it (boiled with baking soda and salt – this being a Japanese custom, proven to reduce some of its toxicities) **on occasion** is relatively safe. However, eating the fern regularly is probably not wise. I also advise against children and women while pregnant (or nursing) eating Bracken fern. Additionally, intestinal upset is not uncommon if excess is consumed at any one sitting.

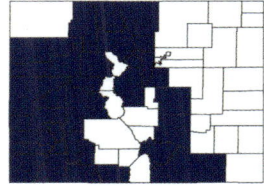

Sustenance Index: Low
Pictured: *Pteridium aquilinum*

Buffalo Gourd
Cucurbita foetidissima

Other Common Names
Missouri gourd, Stinking gourd, Wild gourd

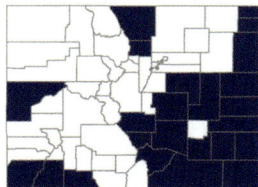

Range & Habitat
Buffalo gourd is occasional throughout the southeastern plains of Colorado. It's most often found growing in exposed and disturbed soils: pastures, old fields, and along roadsides.

Edible Uses
Buffalo gourd should be picked when fully mature (yet still green or just beginning to yellow). Crack the soft-ball–sized gourd open by stepping on it and then remove the seeds. Spread the seeds out on a flat area (the adhering pulp will be removed later) and allow them to dry – a dehydrator or full sun will speed this process. Once dry, rub away any adhering dried gourd pulp. Finally, give the seeds a good water rinse to remove any residual bitterness from the inner gourd pulp.

    With a little oil, lay the seeds out on a baking tray. Bake the seeds in an oven at about 350 degrees until they just begin to brown. They are a good tasting pumpkin seed alternative. Filled with healthful oils (essential fatty acids), minerals, and protein, they make a fine addition to any wild food diet.

Medicinal Uses, Cautions, & Special Note
The ample root, as with most wild gourd types, can be used to make a weak soap solution. Containing large amounts of saponins the dried/fresh root is lathered in water and used for its detergent effect. There are no cautions for the seeds.

    Buffalo gourd belongs to the same family as squash and pumpkin. The crushed leaves really do stink: 'foetidissima'.

Sustenance Index: High

Pictured: *Cucurbita foetidissima (top & circle)* | *C. foetidissima [roasted seeds/raw gourd] (bottom)*

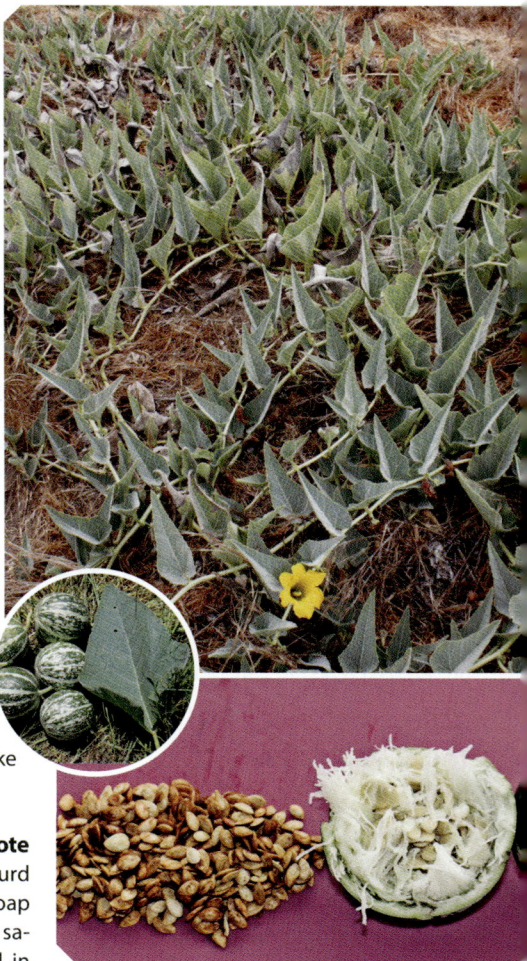

10

Cattail
Typha spp.

Other common names
Punks, Broadleaf cattail, Narrowleaf cattail, Southern cattail, Espadilla

Range & habitat
Cattail is an aquatic plant associated with shallow sections of ponds and lakes. Several species are found in Colorado, however, Broadleaf cattail (Typha latifolia) is the most common.

Edible uses
Utilized worldwide, Cattail is a significant food plant. The young leafing stem (2' or under) is used as a potherb or cooked and added to soups, etc. The older stems are utilized by peeling away the leaves until the inner crisp core is exposed. It is eaten raw or chopped and added to salads, or steamed/sautéed, etc. The immature female flowerheads, or punks, are boiled/cooked and eaten (eat around the tough inner stem). Cattail pollen is collected by banging/shaking the mature male flower clusters in a container. Rich in protein, the pollen is added to other flours in making baked goods (or eaten as a gruel).

   The edible part Cattail root is best procured by cutting away the outer fibrous/spongy parts. The starchy inner core that remains is eaten fresh or cooked. It too can be dried, ground, and shifted, and utilized as a nutritious flour.

Medicinal Uses, Cautions, & Special Note
There are no medicinal uses for Cattail. Before collecting, be sure the plant is growing in a non–contaminated area (see Tule for a sanitizing chlorine bleach soak). Regardless of species, all Cattails can be used alike. Cattail and Tule may be confused by the casual observer (uses are similar, so no harm will come from this). Both are upright water–growing plants, but Cattail has punks and long linear pointed leaves. Tule does not.

Sustenance Index: High
Pictured: *Typha domingensis (top)* | *Typha latifolia [pollen & shaved root core w/ stem] (bottom)*

Checkermallow
Sidalcea candida, S. neomexicana

Other Common Names
White checkerbloom, Rocky Mountain Checkerbloom

Range & Habitat
Throughout Colorado, both species are found at Ponderosa pine–Fir–Spruce–Aspen elevations. Always associated with moist soils, the commonest areas to look for Checkermallow are around springs/seeps, moist meadows, and streamsides.

Sidalcea candida is confined to the Southern Rocky Mountains; outlier populations are found in Utah (and Nevada). S. neomexicana has a wider range. It's found additionally in Oregon, California, and Arizona.

Edible Uses
Belonging to the Mallow family, all parts of Checkermallow are mucilaginous (slimy, like Okra) when crushed or chewed. Mild tasting but hairy, the young leaves (and flowers) are well–used as a salad ingredient or pot–herb. Sautéing or steaming the herbal parts tends to reduce the mucilage factor.

The roots of Sidalcea neomexicana are small and semi–tuberous. Pleasant–tasting, crisp, but somewhat mucilaginous, they make a fine fresh edible – wash and eat. They too are well–suited as a cooked item. In terms of usage, Great Plains growing Winecup (Callirhoe involucrata), also in the Mallow family, is a nearly–identical edible plant.

Medicinal Uses, Cautions, & Special Note
Similar to Marshmallow root, Sidalcea neomexicana's roots, dried and prepared as a tea, are a soothing demulcent/emollient. Checkermallow belongs to the Mallow family – a very safe plant grouping. Sidalcea species are well–known for their leaf dimorphism – shallowly lobed and deeply cleft (upper circle) leaves usually occur on the same plant.

Sustenance Index: Medium
Pictured: *Sidalcea neomexicana*

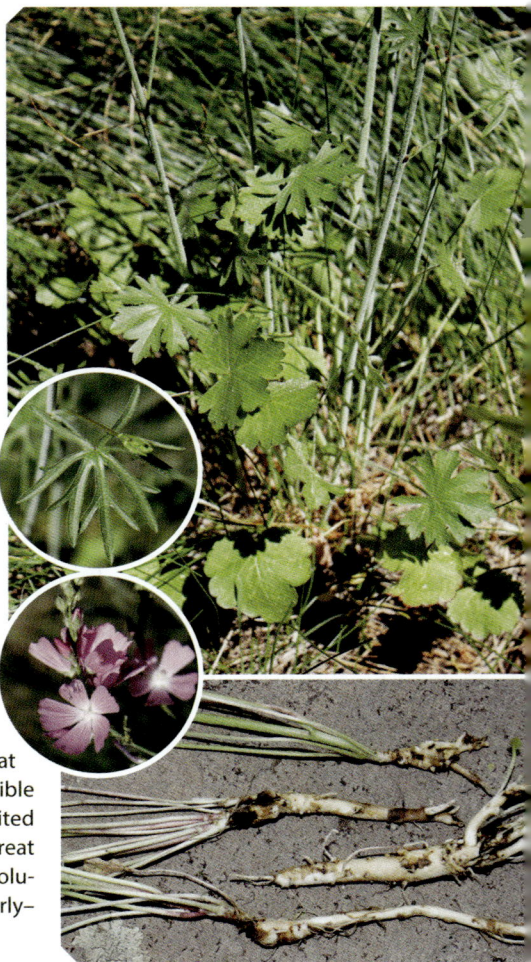

12

Chokecherry
Prunus virginiana var. demissa (P. virginiana var. melanocarpa)

Other Common Names
Western chokecherry

Range & Habitat
The main Chokecherry variety in Colorado is var. demissa (sometimes referred to as var. melanocarpa). It's common to the middle mountains, along moist canyon bottoms and just up from streamsides. In the wild, it tends to be a many–stemmed suckering small tree/shrub.

Edible Uses
Chokecherries are edible freshly picked from the tree or prepared as a jam/jelly. When fully ripe (black) they are sweet and have a very pleasant wild cherry (hint of bitter) flavor. Naturally, the pits (seeds) should first be spit out before the fruit is eaten (or removed if processing for other preparations). Imparting its characteristic flavor, Chokecherry fruit mixes very well with other wild berry combinations.

Bake (important) the pits at 350 degrees for 20 minutes or so. Crack the pit (I use a vise) and eat the kernel within. They are small but pleasant and nutty tasting.

Medicinal Uses, Cautions, & Special Note
The dried bark of Eastern chokecherry (called Wild cherry in the herbal medicine world) is a standard treatment for a dry cough with bronchial inflammation. Western chokecherry is used the same way.

The pits, leaves, and bark contain small amounts of cyanogenic glycosides, common to many Rose family plants. Cooking/heating/drying degrades these compounds. Prior to ripening, Chokecherries are very astringent.

Black cherry (Prunus serotina) is another edible native species of Cherry. It is found further south – AZ, NM, TX, and additionally throughout eastern parts of the country.

Sustenance Index: Medium
Pictured: *Prunus virginiana var. demissa*

Creeping Hollygrape

Berberis repens (Berberis aquifolium var. repens, Mahonia repens)

Other Common Names

Creeping mahonia, Little oregongrape, Oregongrape

Range & Habitat

Common throughout the Rocky Mountains, Creeping hollygrape is found in shady areas with Ponderosa pine, Spruce, and Douglas fir/Fir overhead.

Although abundant throughout all of Colorado's forested ranges, it is absent from low elevation areas and the eastern Plains.

Edible Uses

Ripening from middle to late summer, the small, blue, bloom–covered fruit develop from 6–petaled cup–shaped yellow flowers.

The berries form in clutches and are pleasant tasting: sweet–tart with a hint of bitter. They are fine consumed fresh or can be prepared as a jelly/fruit preserve. Another option is to dehydrate the berries and add them to trail mix and the like.

Medicinal Uses

Creeping hollygrape is a medicinal plant of note. The roots contain significant amounts of isoquinoline alkaloids (berberine, et al.). It's useful for an array of liver, gastrointestinal, and microbial complaints. Most American herbalists utilize this species (or Berberis aquifolium) in some capacity. See *Medicinal Plants of the Western Mountain States* for a full write–up.

Cautions & Special Note

There are no cautions for the fruit. Several related (but less common) plants are found in Colorado. Two Barberry species, Fendler's barberry and Common barberry, which have stem thorns, and one other Hollygrape type, Fremont's mahonia, a large spiny–leaved bush; all have edible berries and similar medicinal uses.

Sustenance Index: Medium

Pictured: *Berberis repens*

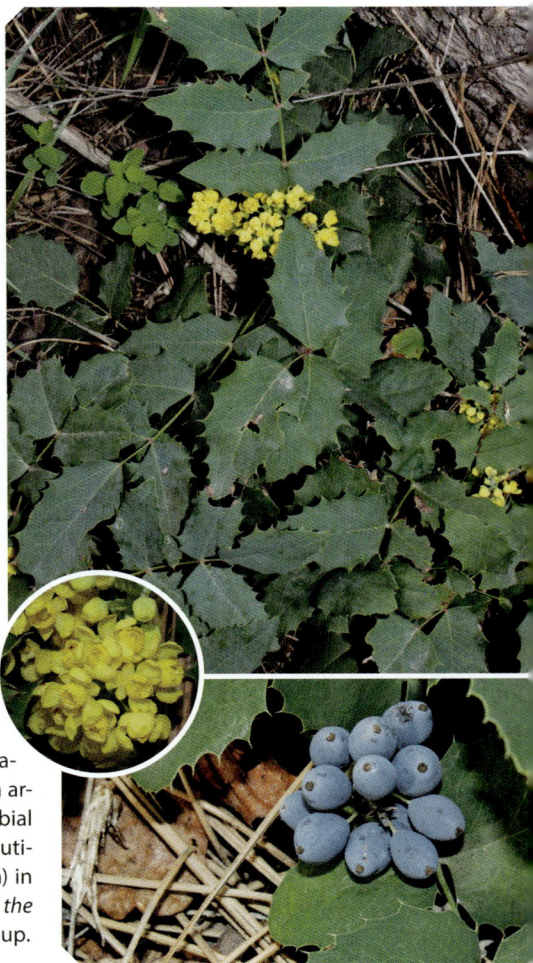

14

Currant

Ribes aureum, R. cereum, R. laxiflorum, R. wolfii

Other Common Names

Golden currant, Wax currant, Trailing black currant, Wolf currant, Clove currant

Range & Habitat

There are no lack of Currant species throughout the southern Rocky Mountain sub–chains of Colorado. Golden currant and Wax currant tend to grow at middle elevations; they are medium–sized bushes. Trailing black currant and Wolf currant are lower–growing and found in the higher mountains around forest openings and drainage sides.

Clove currant (Ribes aureum var. villosum), a variant of Golden currant, makes its way into eastern Colorado's plains and hills.

Edible Uses

Golden currant and Wax currant produce semi–sweet to neutral–tasting berries. Trailing black currant, Wolf currant, and Clove currant with their purple/black fruit are sweeter than the other two. All are fine consumed fresh and also make good jam/jelly candidates. Currant fruit contains fair amounts of vitamin C and health–promoting antioxidant flavonoids.

Medicinal Uses, Cautions & Special Note

Currant leaves are mildly astringent. The fresh leaf poultice is soothing to minor scrapes, insect bites, and sunburn. There are no cautions for Currant.

Gooseberry is also a Ribes. With one exception in Colorado (Gooseberry currant/Ribes montigenum), Gooseberry types have stem/node thorns. Currant types have no stem/node thorns. Uses for both kinds are the same. Native species of Currant are related to European Black currant (Ribes nigrum), which is the source of a commercially popular fruit and essential fatty acid supplement (seeds). *See also Gooseberry.*

Sustenance Index: Medium
Pictured: *Ribes cereum*

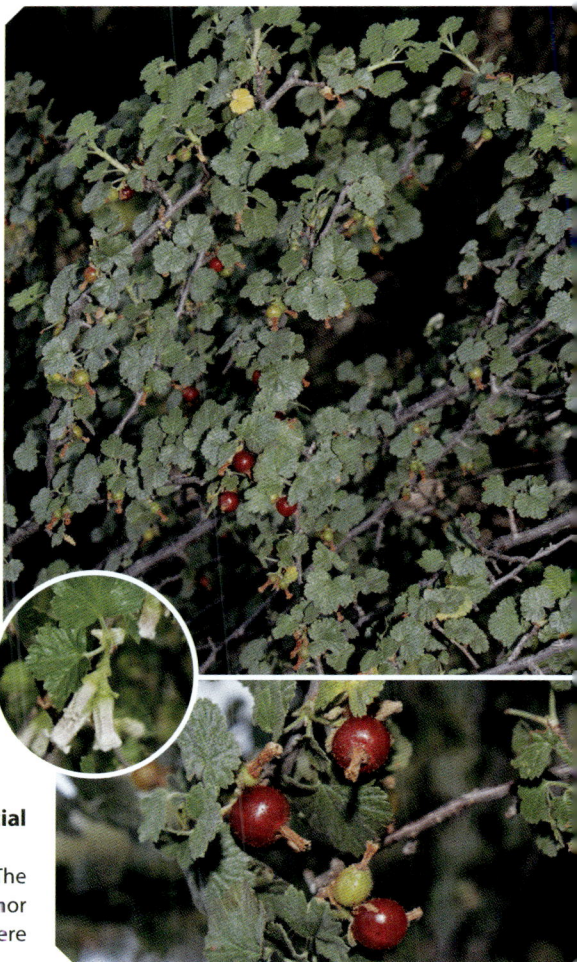

15

Evening Primrose
Oenothera elata ssp. hirsutissima (Oenothera hookeri)

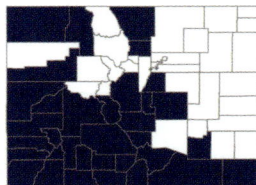

Other Common Names
Hooker's evening primrose, Western evening primrose

Range & Habitat
Hooker's evening primrose grows at about 5000'–8500' throughout much of mountainous Colorado. Almost always found in disturbed soils, road-sides are one of its preferred habitats, though sandy/loamy creek beds and intermittent drainages will be better places to look for uncontaminated plants.

Edible Uses
Late first year or early second year roots (the plant is a biannual) are best for edible uses. Be sure to gather the root when the plant is still a basal rosette of leaves, before it develops a stalk; otherwise the roots will be too woody to utilize. Discard the leaves and chop and boil the roots for 15 minutes (or longer). Drain, rinse, season, and then serve as a vegetable of sorts. Their taste is fair, but texture somewhat fibrous.

The seeds, garbled from the dried pods, can be ground and eaten or sprinkled on salads and the like for their nutritional aspects.

Medicinal Uses
If nothing else is available, use the fresh poulticed herb on rashes, insect bites, and sunburn. It is mildly soothing. The seeds (Oenothera biennis) are a main source for gamma linolenic acid (consider Hooker's evening primrose to be similar). Deficiency of this essential fatty acid has been linked to glandular and inflammatory problems.

Cautions & Special Note
There are no cautions for the plant. Oenothera biennis' (similar to this species) roots were once used in war–torn parts of Europe as a famine food, mostly as a soup ingredient.

Sustenance Index: Medium
Pictured: *Oenothera elata ssp. hirsutissima*

Fairybells

Prosartes trachycarpa (Disporum trachycarpum)

Other Common Names

Rough–fruited fairy–bells. Rough–fruited mandarin

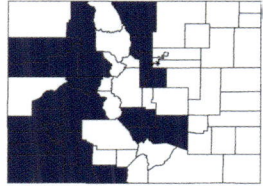

Range & Habitat

Fairybells tends to grow between 8000'–9000' as an understory herbaceous perennial. Commonly found in the shaded and moist soils of coniferous forests, look for it in the state's higher ranges. The plant is widespread but occasional in population density.

Edible Uses

Eat the fruit of Fairybells when immature. They are most appealing prior to ripening. At this point they are greenish–white and taste pleasant and cucumber–like. If allowed to fully ripen (reddish–orange) they become poor–tasting and mushy. Fairybells' best use is as a simple trail snack when encountered.

Medicinal Uses

I am unfamiliar with any medicinal use for Fairybells.

Cautions

There are no cautions for Fairybells.

Special Note

Two similar–appearing plants are often found along with Fairybells. Neither are poisonous; however, I cannot fully attest to their palatability. False Solomon's Seal (Maianthemum racemosum) develops a red berry, but I have found it to be sweet–bitter and unpalatable. Star Solomon's Seal (Maianthemum stellatum) has a green (with blue stripes) berry when immature that turns black when ripe. I have yet to sample Star Solomon's Seal, so am unable to offer an opinion.

Sustenance Index: Medium
Pictured: *Prosartes trachycarpa*

Gambel Oak
Quercus gambelii

Other Common Names
White oak, Rocky Mountain white oak

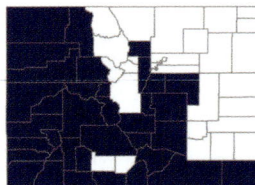

Range & Habitat
Gambel oak is the most abundant Quercus species in Colorado and additionally throughout the Southern Rockies. Ponderosa pine and Aspen are its commonest associates. It's one of the first trees to repopulate after logging or fire.

Edible Uses
The fruit of Gambel oak (any Oak species) is called an acorn. They take one season (White oak type) to mature. When ready in autumn the shell is tan–brown and they begin to fall from the tree. They are collected from the ground or gathered by branch shaking. Only acorns with no worm/insect holes and without damaged shells should be collected. Before processing, be sure they have dried completely (spread out on cardboard/screen). Once dried, crack the acorn's shell and remove the inner 'nutmeat'. Pulverize the nutmeat and hot or cold water leach the meal so no bitterness/astringency remains (change the water every day until no discoloration is visible). The meal–slurry is then dehydrated for later use (it combines well with corn or wheat flours in baking), prepared as a gruel, or shaped (mixed with maple syrup or honey) and dried as a cake. Acorn meal is very nutritious and should have a pleasantly nutty flavor once properly leached.

Medicinal Uses & Cautions
Oak bark is a tannin source (primitive hide tanning). As a skin wash, it reduces tissue redness and irritation. Oak bark tea is imbibed for its anti–diarrheal astringency. Large amounts of improperly leached meal (tannins) may cause stomach upset, constipation, and kidney irritation.

Sustenance Index: High
Pictured: *Quercus gambelii*

18

Gooseberry

Ribes inerme, R. lacustre, P. leptanthum

Other Common Names
Whitestem gooseberry, Black gooseberry, Trumpet gooseberry

Range & Habitat
Colorado is home to three species of Gooseberry. They vary to some degree in distribution, however, the surest habitats for these plants are middle mountain open coniferous forests and forest edges.

Edible Uses
Gooseberries are the size of a small grape/large pea and purple–black when fully ripe. They are fine consumed fresh; also, they make a serviceable jelly base or can be dried and rehydrated for future use. Their seeds are small enough to be eaten unnoticed. Additionally, like most Ribes berries, Gooseberry is high in vitamin C.

Black–fruited species in Colorado (Gooseberry) tend to be sweeter than red–fruited species of Ribes (many Currant species). However they are all equally edible, no matter the berry's color.

Medicinal Uses
Like Currant leaves, Gooseberry leaf is a mild astringent and can be used as a topical soother for minor sunburn, scrapes, and abrasions.

Cautions
There are no cautions for Gooseberry.

Special Note
In Colorado, with one exception (Gooseberry currant/Ribes montigenum, which is a Currant–type with thorns), Ribes species can be separated into one of two groups by whether they have stem/node thorns. If the plant is spiny, then it is a Gooseberry. If the plant is spineless, then it is a Currant. Aside from slight botanical differences, edible (and medicinal) uses for both types are the same.

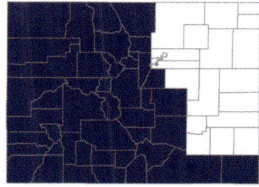

Sustenance Index: Medium
Pictured: *Ribes leptanthum (top & bottom)* | *Ribes inerme (circle)*

19

Greenthread
Thelesperma filifolium, T. megapotamicum, T. subnudum

Other Common Names
Cota, Hopi tea, Indian tea, Navajo tea, Pampa tea

Range & Habitat
Three species of Greenthread grow throughout Colorado. Absent from the mountains, they are inhabitants of the eastern Plains and drier middle elevations of the western part of the state. The sandy soil of dirt roadsides, flats, and slopes are some typical places to look for Greenthread.

Thelesperma megapotamicum is likely the most widely–used species. It's additionally the easiest to recognize with its unusually large–bulbous flower head.

Edible Uses
Greenthread is a traditional Hopi and Navajo tea plant (and other tribes). Not particularly medicinal, the herbal infusion is simply imbibed as a pleasant–tasting beverage. Mild and non–bitter, it's sipped alone, or mixed with other herbs as part of a combination.

Not a well–known use: the very–young leaves, when first emerging from the ground, before stem development, are gathered, chopped, and added fresh to salads and the like as an accent/garnish.

Medicinal Uses & Cautions
Greenthread is a mild diuretic. There are no cautions for Greenthread.

Special Note
The foliage and roots (Thelesperma megapotamicum) were once processed to form a yellow–brown pigment. Thelesperma filifolium and T. subnudum develop both disc and ray florets (flower petals). T. megapotamicum has disc florets only.

Sustenance Index: Low
Pictured: *Thelesperma megapotamicum (top & bottom)* | *Thelesperma subnudum (circle)*

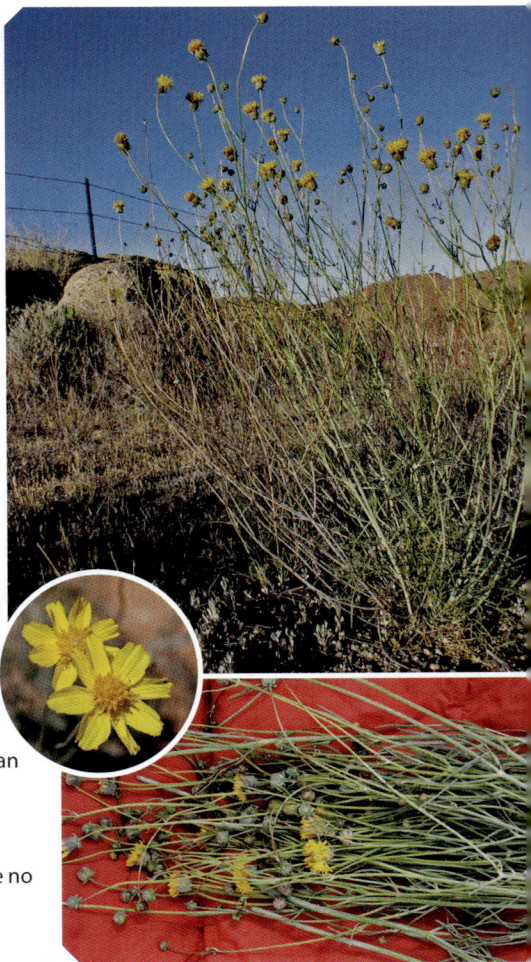

20

Ground Cherry

Physalis spp.

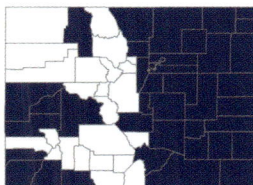

Other Common Names

Tomatillo, Husk tomato, Ivyleaf ground cherry, Longleaf ground cherry

Range & Habitat

Colorado is home to a handful of Ground cherry species. They prefer disturbed soils: dirt road and trail sides, field sides, canyon bottoms, and draws. Look for Ground cherry on the eastern Plains or in desert regions.

Edible Uses

Usually ripening from late summer to fall, each fruit is encased in an inflated sac. Depending on species, the fruit are greenish–tan to yellowish–orange (occasionally darker) when ripe.

Be sure to remove the 'cherry' from its encasement before eating. They taste sweetish–acidic and tomato–like. If immature, they are better cooked. When ripe, eat raw or combine them with other wild edibles. Ground cherry tastes good enough to be substituted for tomatoes in salsa

Medicinal Uses

Due to small amounts of solanine, the foliage is potentially drying to the gastrointestinal tract and ocular/nasal regions (prepared as a tincture or tea).

Cautions

Although there are no cautions for the ripe fruit, the foliage may produce a toxic reaction if ingested (greater than medicinal [small] quantities).

Special Note

Some may confuse other wild Nightshades (Solanum spp.) with Ground cherry. Unlike Ground cherry, the fruit of Solanum species have no sac. Most Solanum species are toxic.

Sustenance Index: Medium
Pictured: *Physalis hederifolia (top & bottom)* | *Physalis longifolia (circle)*

Hawthorn
Crataegus erythropoda, C. rivularis

Other Common Names
Cerro Hawthorn, River hawthorn

Range & Habitat
Hawthorn is a small tree with toothed leaves, 5–petaled white flowers, and red fruit. Overlapping in range throughout Colorado, both species are found at Ponderosa–Aspen–Oak elevations, usually in association with drainages. Look for Hawthorn along stream and canyon sides and on slopes/hillsides just up from ponds/lakes/reservoirs.

Edible Uses
Ripening mid to late summer, Hawthorn berries are fairly sweet, however, seed–filled. Aside from mouthing a few berries at a time (and spitting out the seeds), the fruit's best use is as a jelly base.

The berries are rich in vitamin C, B vitamins, and various antioxidants.

Medicinal Uses
Although Hawthorn can be considered edible, it's better thought of as first being medicinal. The fruit, flowers, and young leaves are a time–honored cardiovascular medicine. Herbal preparations are extensively–researched, well–tolerated, and effectively applied towards low–level (pre–surgical intervention) heart complaints. High blood pressure and poor valvular function are two main indications that point to Hawthorn's use. Colorado's species are similar in chemistry and therefore use to the better known European species.

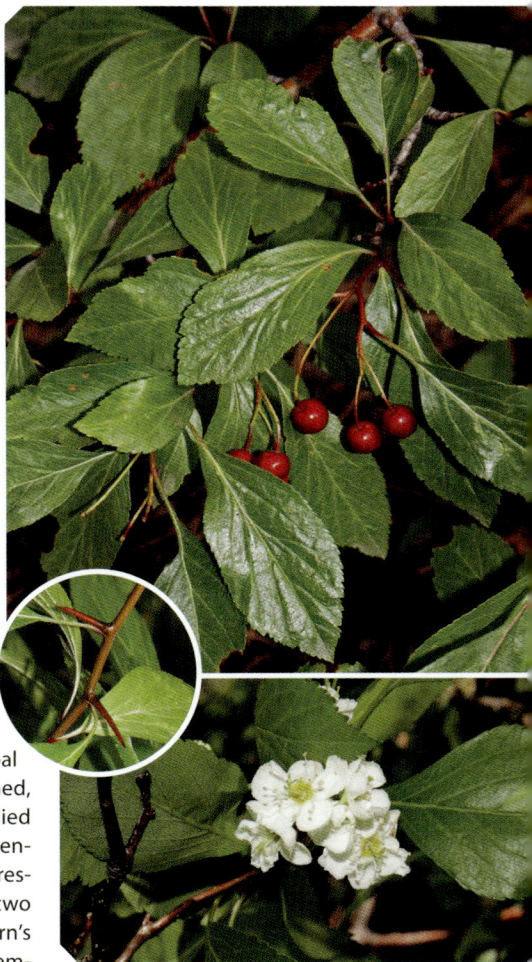

Cautions & Special Note
Hawthorn in caution–free. The plant is related to Rose (Rose hips), Serviceberry, and Raspberry.

Sustenance Index: Medium
Pictured: *Crataegus rivularis*

Heartleaf Bittercress
Cardamine cordifolia

Other Common Names
Large mountain bittercress

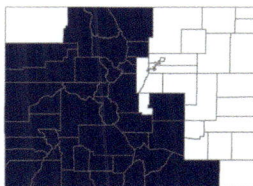

Range & Habitat
A prolific Rocky Mountain grower, in Colorado Heartleaf bittercress is common to the majority of ranges.

Look for the plant along streamsides and on moist meadows/hillsides (with Aspen and conifers overhead).

Edible Uses
A fair–tasting Wild mustard type, the young leafing–flowering tops are the plant's best part. Eat this portion fresh (limited), or in larger amounts once streamed/sautéed.

Added to other cooked greens, Heartleaf bittercress provides a nice spicy–mustard (hint of bitter) accent.

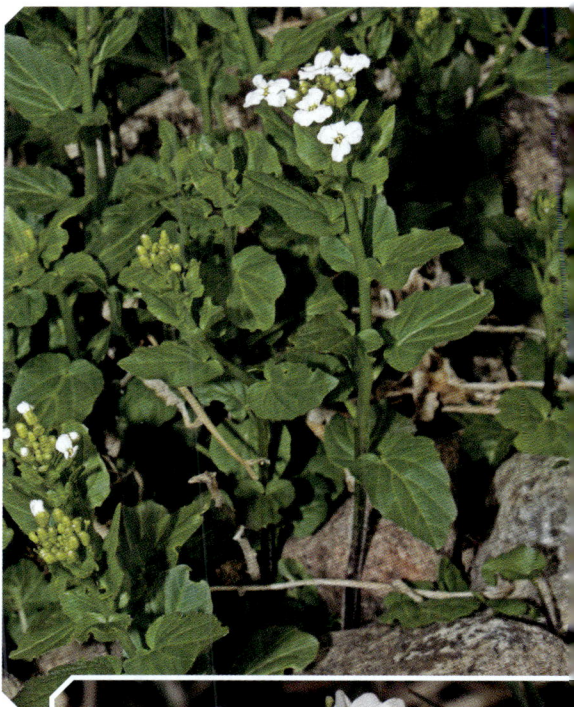

Medicinal Uses
Glucosinolates are a group of volatile compounds common to the Mustard family. These compounds are responsible for Heartleaf bittercress' spicy and stimulating properties.

Eat a small handful of the fresh leaf if suffering from indigestion and/ or bloating.

Cautions
I've observed large amounts of related Mustard family plants cause stomach upset and for women, stimulate menses.

Special Note
Heartleaf bittercress is related to Watercress, Wintercress, and the vegetables, cabbage, broccoli, brussels sprouts, and others. They are all members of the Mustard family.

Sustenance Index: Low
Pictured: *Cardamine cordifolia*

23

Indian Rice Grass

Achnatherum hymenoides (Oryzopsis hymenoides, Stipa hymenoides)

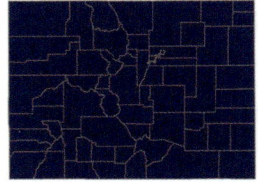

Other Common Names
Indian mountain ricegrass, Indian millet, Silky mountain rice

Range & Habitat
A middle elevation bunch grass, Indian rice grass is especially common throughout Colorado. It is found state–wide and represented in every county.

    Well–drained and sun–exposed hillsides, slopes, and flats, with occasional Juniper and Pinyon, are some ideal locations for Indian rice grass.

Edible Uses
The seed is gathered from late spring through early fall – lower elevation plants flower/fruit earlier than higher elevation ones. Lightly pinch with thumb and forefinger below a fruiting panicle; then gently pull, stripping the seed away from the stem. Place the seed in a paper bag and repeat.

    Set the seed aside for 1–2 weeks so it dries completely. One de–chaffing technique for small amounts is to simply rub a bunch between hands several feet above a container in a light breeze (or a fan set on low). Slowly let the seed/chaff fall. The breeze will take away the chaff while the heavier seed drops into the container. Keep repeating this process until only the grain remains.

    Another way is to parch the seed, so the fuzzy chaff is burnt away (bottom photo). Prepare Indian ricegrass like any other seed/grain: cooked whole, as a flour or meal, etc.

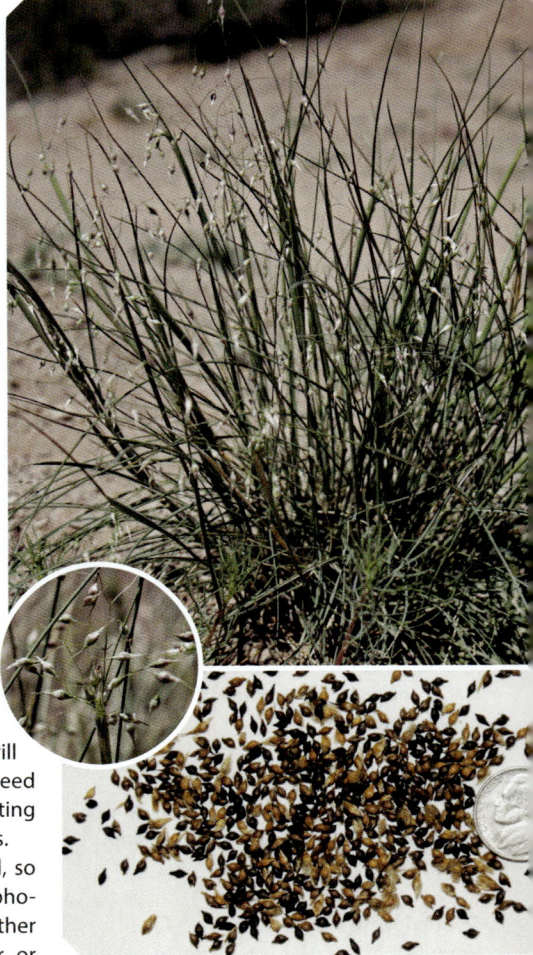

Medicinal Uses, Cautions, & Special Note
There are no medicinal uses/cautions for Indian rice grass. Before corn arrived on the scene, the plant was a main grain staple of the western Indians. The plant's commonality and seed size (for a native grass, it's one of the largest) made it a valuable and much utilized edible.

Sustenance Index: High
Pictured: *Achnatherum hymenoides*

Lambsquarters
Chenopodium spp.

Other Common Names
Goosefoot, Quelites, Chual

Range & Habitat
Lambsquarters species are common throughout Colorado. The plant does well in disturbed soils: roadsides, trail-sides, cattle tank areas, etc.

Edible Uses
The plant's young leaves are the most palatable part; with age they often become a little acrid. For the consumption of moderate to large quantities, the leaves should first be boiled, then rinsed. Most species are high in calcium and vitamin A. The seeds of Lambsquarters (related to Amaranth) too are a good food source. They are gathered and winnowed once the plant starts to bolt; after which they are ground into a meal or simply added to and/or cooked with other foods.

Medicinal Uses
Epazote (Chenopodium [Dysphania] ambrosioides) is the main medicinal species of the genus. It is not found in the wild (Colorado), but on occasion it is cultivated in the garden. A spice and useful carminative, Epazote also smells and tastes differently than Lambsquarters when crushed fresh, like restroom disinfectant.

Cautions & Special Note
Kidney stone suffers may find that eating large amounts of the fresh plant (daily) will contribute to this condition (due to a high oxalate content). There is no problem with Lambsquarters as an occasional edible. Chenopodium album (both native and non–native varieties) is the main edible Lambsquarters species. It is somewhat common in Colorado. However, C. berlandieri and C. fremontii are more regionally abundant. They all have identical edible uses. Generally, wider–leaf species are more palatable than thin–leaf species.

Sustenance Index: Medium
Pictured: *Chenopodium album (top)* | *C. incanum (bottom)*

Lemonade Berry
Rhus aromatica

Other Common Names
Squawbush, Skunkbush, Three–leaved sumac

Range & Habitat
Colorado is home to two species of Lemonade berry. R. aromatica and Rhus glabra. Of the two plants, R. aromatica is far more common. It is found throughout middle elevations, nearly state–wide.

Edible Uses
Lemonade berry's ripe fruit are red, sticky, and lemon–sour tasting. Once gathered, a pleasantly tart and re-freshing tea can be made from the fruit. This process, whether a sun–tea or a hot water infusion, is Lemonade berry's best preparation. The sun tea is an easy enough process: infuse 1oz of berries in 1qt of water. Let the mix-ture stand for at least several hours, then strain and sweeten the tea to taste.

   Although not Lemonade berry's best use, the fruit can simply be eaten as is (better sucked on and then spit out) – they are mealy and dry.

Medicinal Uses & Cautions
The leaves are astringent and can be used as a soothing poultice for burns, scrapes, and abrasions. The fruit is caution–free.

Special Note
All other red–fruited Rhus species can be used like Lemonade berry. The fruit of most species contain small amounts of vitamin C – approximately 2–3 milligrams per ounce.

   Related Poison ivy/Poison sumac have a white–milky sap when a stem or leaf is broken (Lemonade berry has no milky sap). Also, unlike the red fruit of Lemonade berry, Poison ivy and Poison sumac have fruit that are greenish–cream in color.

Sustenance Index: Low
Pictured: *Rhus aromatica*

26

Mallow
Malva neglecta

Other Common Names
Common mallow, Cheeseweed, Cheeseplant

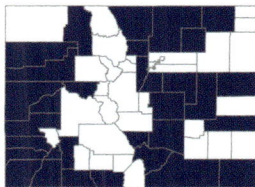

Range & Habitat
Encountered throughout middle to upper elevations (4500'–3500'), Mallow will almost always be found in disturbed soils: dirt roadsides, walkway edges, old grades, fallow fields, etc. It responds aggressively to seasonal rains and is visible (and collectible) from late spring to summer.

Edible Uses
The leaves, being the most palatable part of Mallow, are simply eaten raw or mixed with other greens as a salad. Really though, they are better boiled or steamed. With added butter and seasoning, most find them similar to cooked spinach. They'll be a little mucilaginous/slimy (Mallow is related to Okra), but still mild tasting and nutritious.

Although the leaf tea does have some medicinal application, it is pleasant enough to be used as a beverage.

Medicinal Uses
The leaves make a soothing tea for sore throats and coughs. It's particularly useful when suffering from a cold or flu, due to Mallow's immune–stimulating polysaccharide content.

Cautions
There are no cautions for Mallow.

Special Note
Malva parviflora (Little mallow) is another species of edible Mallow. Unlike M. neglecta, it is found at lower elevations throughout Southwest (absent from most of Colorado). Mallow is closely related to Checkermallow (Sidalcea), in fact both species should be treated the same in terms of edibility (foliage).

Sustenance Index: Low
Pictured: *Malva neglecta*

Mariposa Lily
Calochortus gunnisonii, C. nuttallii

Other Common Names
Gunnison's mariposa lily, Sego lily

Range & Habitat
The epicenter of the Calochortus genus is California, where dozens of species exist. In Colorado, two main plants are present – Calochortus gunnisonii (Gunnison's mariposa lily) and C. nuttallii (Sego lily). Both species are found on slopes, gradual hillsides, and flats. Gunnison's mariposa lily is a higher–elevation grower, mainly associated with forest meadows. C. nuttallii is common throughout the high desert and scrub–lands of western parts of the state.

Edible Uses
From flower and stem to bulb, all parts of Mariposa lily are edible. The buds, flowers, young seed pods, stems, and leaves can be eaten without killing the plant. They are pleasant tasting and have a mild nutty flavor.

The bulbs require more effort to procure. They are often ½' or so beneath the ground's surface, so the utilization of a digging implement will be necessary. The bulbs provide more sustenance due to their greater carbohydrate content. They too are pleasant tasting (but starchy). Eat them raw or cooked.

Medicinal Uses & Cautions
Mariposa lily has no medicinal use nor are there cautions associated with the plant.

Special Note
Be sure the population at hand is abundant – two species in southwestern Colorado are at their range's edge (Calochortus flexuosus and C. aureus). All species are only identifiable for 2–4 weeks when it is in flower/seed. After this window has passed, its above–ground trace is gone until next year.

Sustenance Index: High
Pictured: *Calochortus nuttallii*

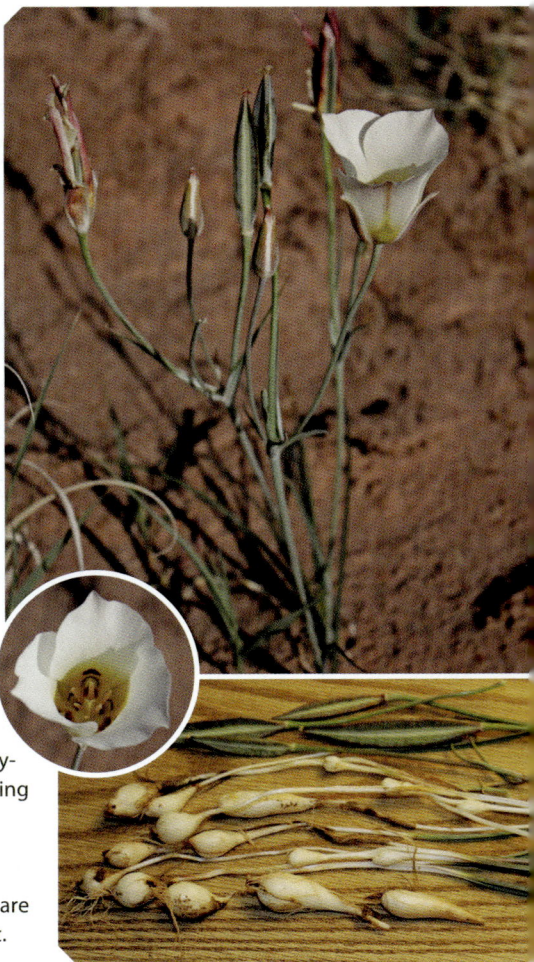

28

Marsh Marigold
Caltha leptosepala

Other Common Names
White marsh marigold, Elkslip

Range & Habitat
A alpine–subalpine plant, Marsh marigold is found in water–logged soils surrounding streams, bogs, fens, marshes, springs, and seeps. Look for it in the Park, Front, and Sawatch Ranges, Sangre de Cristos and San Juans. It's absent from the high desert, middle lands, and eastern Plains.

Edible Uses
Gather the just–forming leaves, stems, and/or flower buds in the spring (or early summer), prior to the plant becoming aged and fibrous. Collected early–on, the herbaceous parts are thickened and semi–succulent. Simmer these parts for 10–15 minutes (important) and rinse with fresh water. Serve as a cooked spinach–like green. The flower buds are pickled like capers (be sure to give them a quick water boil and rinse prior to a brine addition). Cooking is important for Marsh marigold – heat dissipates its irritating lactone content (see Cautions).

Medicinal Uses & Cautions
In small amounts, fresh Marsh marigold is used as an internal/topical tissue stimulant. *See Medicinal Plants of the Western Mountain States.*

Eaten fresh, Marsh marigold can be irritating to oral and gastric tissues, producing a very acrid/burning sensation. This is due to the plant's lactone content. Heat (simmering) quickly dissipates this irritating principle. Additionally, one chemical study found that Marsh marigold contains the toxic alkaloid, senecionine. This is likely an erroneous finding, since it has never been duplicated and pyrrolizidine alkaloids for the Buttercup family are virtually non–existent. However, just in case, eat (well–cooked and rinsed) Marsh marigold just on occasion as a seasonal delicacy and not as a staple.

Sustenance Index: Low
Pictured: *Caltha leptosepala*

Monkey Flower
Mimulus guttatus (Erythranthe guttata)

Other Common Names
Yellow monkey flower, Common monkey flower, Seep monkey flower

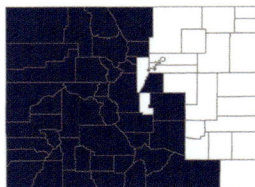

Range & Habitat
Surprisingly variable in elevation, Monkey flower is always found around (or directly in) water. Creeks, springs, and seeps reliably host the plant – lake/pond sides, not so much.

Entirely a plant of western North America, Monkey flower is absent from the Plains and eastward.

Edible Uses
Monkey flower makes for a fair–tasting early springtime green. The young leaves, before the plant's stem and flowers develop, is the choice edible part. At this time, the leaves are eaten raw, or boiled/steamed and consumed as a cooked green. Their taste is like mildly bitter lettuce.

Further along in the season, when Monkey flower becomes a mature plant, it can still be eaten raw, but is often too bitter to be consumed in any quantity. Boiling the leaf, then following up with a quick rinse will remove some of its bitterness, allowing greater amounts to be eaten.

Medicinal Uses & Cautions
There are no medicinal uses or cautions for Monkey flower.

Special Note
Monkey flower may be confused with Watercress when young and not in flower (both plants grow in water). Taste a leaf – if bland yet a little bitter, it is Monkey flower; if mustard–spicy, then Watercress. Mimulus glabratus (Roundleaf monkey flower) is another common species. It grows in similar habitats; however, it is smaller and generally prostrate. It is utilized like Mimulus guttatus.

Sustenance Index: Low
Pictured: *Mimulus guttatus*

Mountain Parsley
Pseudocymopterus montanus (Cymopterus lemmonii)

Other Common Names
Alpine false springparsley

Range & Habitat
A small perennial of the Southern Rocky Mountains, Mountain parsley is abundant throughout all of Colorado's upper elevation ranges. Associated with conifers, especially Ponderosa pine, look for Mountain parsley in open forests, meadows, and other full–partial sun exposures.

Edible Uses
Consider Mountain parsley one of the top–ten wild edibles to know in the mountains. The entire plant is utilizable and since the root is the main part, it provides more sustenance than many other plants. The roots: tender taproots that shred easily, they usually are unbranched and reach 1'–2' deep. Eat them fresh or chop and cook as needed. The above–ground foliage is also edible, fresh or cooked. One way to enjoy Mountain parsley is to snip and eat the flowers while hiking through a patch. All parts have a faint but agreeable fresh–mild carrot/parsley smell and taste.

Medicinal Uses, Cautions, & Special Note
There are no medicinal uses or cautions for Mountain parsley. Two deadly plants, Poison hemlock (PH) and Water hemlock (WH) are related to Mountain parsley (MP). Here are some important differences: leaflet veins of WH travel to the cut (between teeth). Veins of MP travel to the tip. WH grows in or on the edge of water. MP does not. WH and PH are much larger than MP (only 1'–2'). PH prefers moist and disturbed soils. MP prefers drier and better–established soils. PH grows lower (usually) in elevation than MP. If still in doubt, wait for MP to flower: WH and PH have white flowers; MP has yellow, or sometimes red–orange flowers.

Sustenance Index: High
Pictured: *Pseudocymopterus montanus*

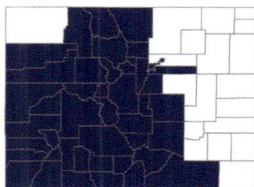

31

Mullein
Verbascum thapsus

Other Common Names
Woolly mullein, Gordolobo

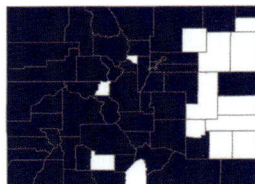

Range & Habitat
Mullein is a biannual, non–native weed. Exceedingly common to Ponderosa pine elevations, it's found almost always in disturbed soils – roadsides, trailsides, and fire–swept areas.

Edible Uses
Select a second–year plant in early to mid–summer. Clip the last 8"–12" of flexible flowering stalk and carefully remove the adhering flower buds and outer rough layer. What's left will be a tender and pliable inner stem, somewhat thinner than a pencil.

The inner stem is eaten raw or once cooked and seasoned. Having an asparagus–like taste and texture, use it as a dish by itself or in combination with other wild foods. Given that entire mountain sides (after a fire) are often covered by hundreds of plants, Mullein is an often over–looked but very abundant wild food that takes only a small amount of effort to process.

Medicinal Uses
Mullein leaf is a standard herbal treatment for a dry hacky cough. The root is used for urinary irritations, and the flower, prepared as an oil, is a soothing earache treatment.

Cautions
There are no cautions for Mullein.

Special Note
Mullein is occasionally referred to as 'toilet–paper plant' by campers due to its leaf size and softness. Proceed at your own risk...itchy!

Sustenance Index: Medium
Pictured: *Verbascum thapsus*

Nettle
Urtica dioica ssp. gracilis

Other Common Names
Stinging nettle, California nettle

Range & Habitat
Urtica dioica ssp. gracilis is really the only Nettle species in Colorado, though ssp. holosericea is found in Moffat County, but just barely. Some surveys list a small group of Urtica gracilenta in Mineral County. If true, these plants should be considered rare.

Look for Nettle at forest elevations, next to streams, drainages, and similar moist and shady areas. Scarcity of plants is not an issue with Nettle. It tends to be rhizomal–colony oriented.

Edible Uses
The ideal time to gather Nettle for food is when it is first forming in the spring, prior to its becoming fibrous and coarse. It is important to simmer/boil Nettle for 5–10 minutes, sometimes longer depending on the coarseness/age of the plant. This softens the herb and renders the stinging hairs inert. Once boiled, Nettle has the consistency of most other cooked wild greens. It is non–bitter and nutritious.

Medicinal Uses, Cautions, & Special Note
Nettle leaf tea is a mineral–rich and alkalizing beverage. The tea also is soothing to urinary irritations and calming to rhinitis/hayfever. Wear gloves/long sleeves when collecting Nettle due to the plant's stinging hairs (trichomes). If stung, the weal (welt) subsides in 30–60 minutes; nevertheless, it is mildly to moderately painful. If Nettle greens are not cooked sufficiently some mouth/throat irritation may occur from improperly neutralized trichomes. Prior to Cotton's dominance, Nettle's fibrous stems (similar to Hemp) were once a base material for cloths, tents, bags, etc.

Sustenance Index: Low
Pictured: *Urtica dioica ssp. gracilis*

Orach

Atriplex dioica, A. hortensis, A. micrantha, A. rosea, A. patula

Other Common Names

Halberdleaf orach, Garden orach, Russian orach, Tumbling orach, Spear orach

Range & Habitat

Generally, the Orach (also spelled Orache) species of Atriplex are annual, fast–growing, leafy, and non–native (Eurasia). Colorado is home to five (more–or–less) such plants, with Atriplex rosea (Tumbling orach) being the most common. Look for these species in ditches, next to culverts, edges of secondary roadsides, and similar moist/disturbed soils. They germinate and grow quickly in response to seasonal rains.

Edible Uses

Related to Amaranth and Lambsquarters, botanically and in use, consider Orach a low–level edible. The young /just–forming leaves are eaten fresh in small amounts. However, they are best simmered/rinsed and consumed as a spinach–like vegetable. I've yet to sample the seeds, but it is said they are somewhat edible and similar to what Lambsquarters' provides.

Medicinal Uses, Cautions, & Special Note

There are no medicinal uses for Orach. Most species of Atriplex harbors moderate to high levels of oxalates; accordingly, be sure to simmer/rinse the leaves before eating large to moderate amounts.

    The perennial species of Atriplex are generally referred to as Saltbush. These plants tend to accumulate sodium, particularly on leaf surfaces. Inversely, most Orach types are not especially salty.

    Even though it has only been in America for two to three hundred years, the Navajo are reported to have used Tumbling orach as an edible in times of scarcity (leaves and seeds) and livestock fodder.

Sustenance Index: Low
Pictured: *Atriplex rosea*

34

Ox–Eye Daisy
Leucanthemum vulgare

Other Common Names
Great ox–eye, Field daisy, Maudlin daisy

Range & Habitat
An abundant non–native plant, Ox–eye daisy grows throughout Colorado's mountain ranges. Mainly found between 8000'–10000', look to dirt roadsides, open meadows, and forest edges with full sun exposures.

Edible Uses
Gather the basal leaves early in the season before the plant develops a flowering stalk. At this point they will be slightly thickened and tender. Fresh, they have a mild taste and are fine used as a garnish or salad addition. Larger amounts should be boiled/sautéed and seasoned accordingly. Ox–eye daisy's caloric content (low) is similar to other leafy greens, so it should be thought of as an addition or garnish food, not a staple.

Medicinal Uses
The dried upper herb (flower and leaf), prepared as a tea is a mild child–safe sudorific/sedative, similar to Chamomile in effect.

Cautions
There are no cautions for Ox–eye daisy.

Special Note
A number of other Leucanthemum/Chrysanthemum species (i.e Chrysanthemum cinerariaefolium or Dalmatian daisy) contain pyrethrins, a group of naturally occurring compounds with well–documented insecticidal properties. These compounds also tend to be mildly to moderately toxic when ingested in sufficient quantities. There are no consistent reports of Ox–eye daisy containing these compounds, at least in greater than trace amounts.

Sustenance Index: Low
Pictured: *Leucanthemum vulgare*

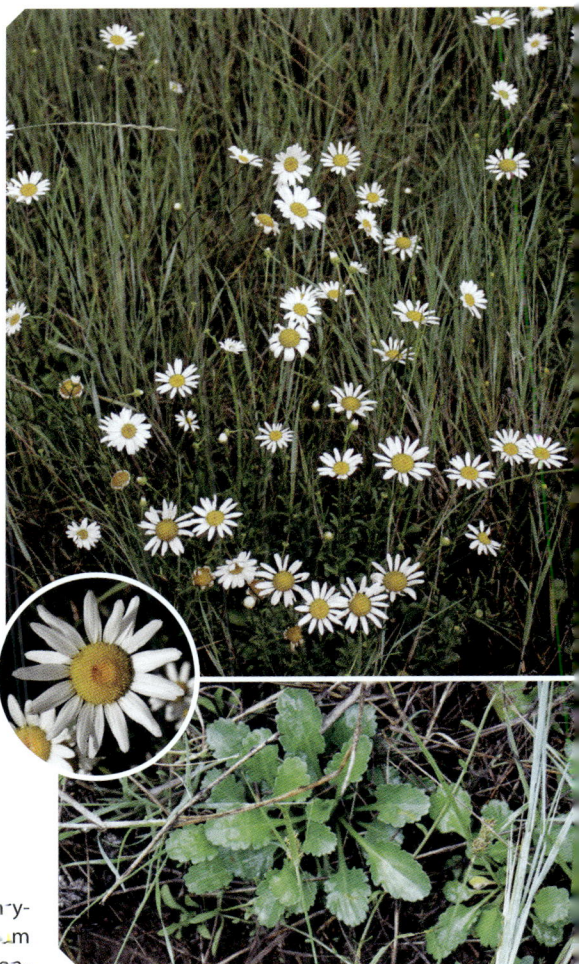

Panicgrass
Panicum capillare

Other Common Names
Common panicgrass, Witchgrass, Ticklegrass, Tumble panic

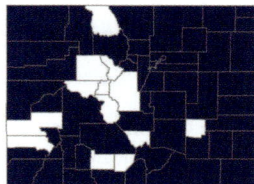

Range & Habitat
A widespread North American annual grass, Panicum capillare is the most commonly encountered species in Colorado (and America).

Throughout mountainous parts of the state, look for the plant from 5000'–8000'. Further to the east it grows lower in elevation. Moist and disturbed soils are its preferred conditions.

Edible Uses
Snip the entire panicle (with 2"–3" of stem) from the grass in late August – too soon and the seeds will not be mature; too late and they will have fallen.

Place the panicles in a paper bag and set them aside for about a week. Strip the seeds from the stems by pinching low on the bunch and pulling towards the top. And/or the panicles can be rolled between the hands. Give the seeds (and small stems) a vigorous hand–rubbing and then winnow them in a light breeze (or fan on low).

Panicgrass is small enough to the eaten unprocessed, so enjoy the whole seed (crunchy–mildly nutty) solo, or sprinkled on salads, meat, etc. They too are fine for flour/meal/gruel/sun–dried cakes. Nutritious, they contain good amounts of protein, carbohydrates, and fats.

Medicinal Uses, Cautions, & Special Note
There are no medicinal uses or cautions for Panicgrass. Like most Panicum species, this plant provided an important nutritional source in primitive times.

Sustenance Index: High
Pictured: *Panicum capillare*

36

Pinyon Pine
Pinus edulis (Pinus cembroides var. edulis)

Other Common Names
Two–needle pinyon, Colorado pinyon, New Mexico pinyon

Range & Habitat
Pinus edulis is the main Pinyon species of the Southwest. It is found as far north as northern Colorado/southern Wyoming. Look for this small–stocky Pine tree on slopes, plateaus, and mesas, often with Juniper, just below Ponderosa pine elevations.

Edible Uses
Pinyon pine seeds (or 'nuts') are larger than other Pine species, which makes them a worthwhile wild food. During the summer, while still green, throw the cones in a campfire (or use a barbecue grill/large wok), watching for them to begin to open. Once expanded by the heat, let them cool a little and remove the seeds. Tear away the thin shell (it should be pliable at this point) and eat the fresh inner seed. Late summer–early fall remove the mature seeds from the cone. Use a nutcracker or a gentle hammer tap to split the shell. Consume the seed freely. They are very nutritious, fine–tasting, and need no preparation, aside from shelling. Pinyon pine seeds are the wild American version of European pine nuts found in commerce.

Medicinal Uses, Cautions, & Special Note
Pine pitch (Pine sap) is antibacterial and can be used internally in small amounts (as a tincture) for bronchial, urinary, and intestinal infections or used topically (diluted) for skin infections. Pine needles and the inner bark contain small amounts of vitamin C. An infusion of the dried green needles makes a good cold and flu tea. Used undiluted, Pine pitch is a tissue irritant (and is flammable). The pitch also can be used as a primitive patching material and sealant.

Sustenance Index: High
Pictured: *Pinus edulis (top & circle)* | *Pinus cembroides (bottom)*

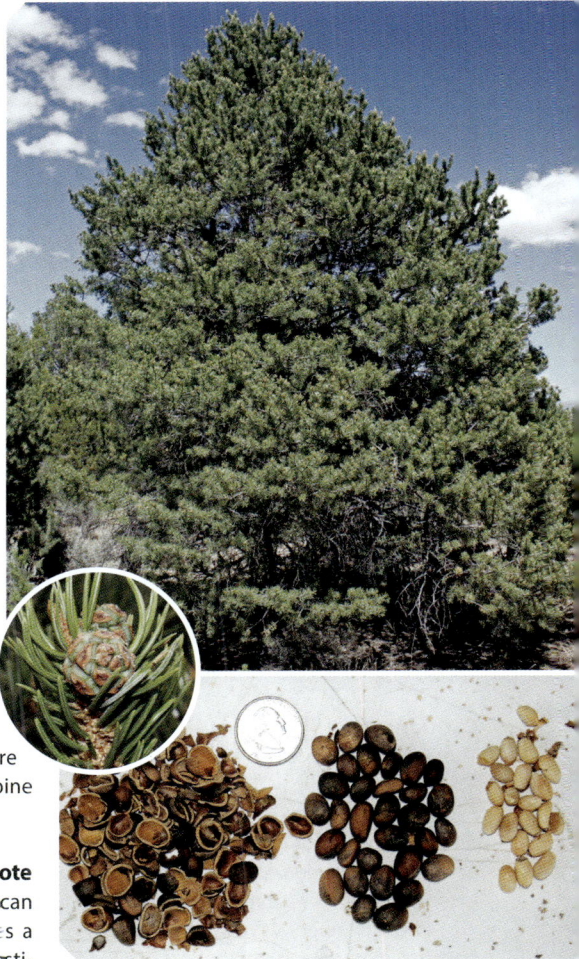

37

Plantain
Plantago major

Other Common Names
Common plantain, Lanté

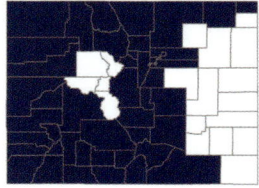

Range & Habitat
Plantain is a non–native short–lived perennial. Absent from drier desert regions, look for the plant in moist and disturbed soils such as trailsides, meadows, and streamsides (and even untended lawns). It's a plant that is encountered with little searching.

Edible Uses
Plantain is entirely edible, yet the young springtime leaves are the choice part. They can be eaten fresh, but most find them better as a cooked green. Sautéed, boiled, or steamed, the leaves are fair–tasting and can be eaten alone, or added to other wild foods.

Medicinal Uses
A mild plant medicine, Plantain is simply used topically as a soothing vulnerary. Internally, as a tea or fresh juice, it is antiinflammatory and heal-ing to gastrointestinal ulcerations.

Cautions
There are no cautions for Plantain.

Special Note
All other species of Plantain are edible (or at least not poisonous), though this species is considered more palatable than others.

    Psyllium fiber, a common over–the–counter dietary supplement, is derived from the seed/seed husk of Plantago ovata. Plantain is unrelated to the cooking type of plantain (Musa spp.). The latter is a type of ba-nana that is often used in Mexican cuisine.

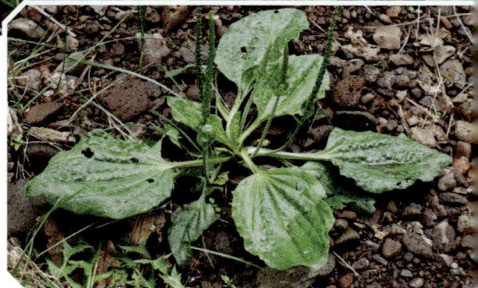

Sustenance Index: Low
Pictured: *Plantago major*

Prickly Pear

Opuntia macrorhiza, O. phaeacantha

Other Common Names

Twist–spine prickly pear, Western prickly pear, Brown–spined prickly pear

Range & Habitat

Colorado hosts a number of Prickly pear species; however, the two main edible fruit–bearing species are Opuntia macrorhiza and O. phaeacantha. They are found at middle/low elevations in dry–soil/exposed habitats.

Edible Uses

Twist–spine prickly pear and Brown–spined prickly pear have sweet (more–or–less) and seed–filled fruit. The flesh is the best portion, but the seeds can be eaten as well. To eat raw, simply slice the fruit open when ripe and scoop out the inner flesh (with seeds) and consume as is. Be sure to not eat the outer fruit skin due to the abundance of tiny thorns (glochids). The fruit also serves as a good jelly, jam, or juice base. The young pads (of any species) can be eaten raw in limited quantities; if cooked, then in larger amounts. They have the taste of a slimy bell pepper. As a cooked vegetable (nopalitos), they are traditionally served with eggs for breakfast (be sure to first remove the thorns and glochids). The pads can also be pickled.

Medicinal Uses, Cautions & Special Note

The inner pad as a poultice is soothing to burns, scrapes, and stings. Internally all parts will slightly lower blood sugar and cholesterol levels. Excessive raw fruit consumption may cause digestive upset; too much raw pad may cause fever, chills, and digestive upset, collectively known as 'Cactus fever'. The pads contain high levels of calcium oxalate. If consuming large amounts (or long term) be sure to boil–rinse the pads. Warning – all parts are covered by tiny thorns, known as glochids, which are very irritating if accidentally rubbed into the eyes (or mouthed–ingested).

Sustenance Index: High

Pictured: *Opuntia phaeacantha (top)* | *O. engelmannii (bottom)*

Purslane
Portulaca oleracea

Other Common Names
Common purslane, Little hogweed, Verdolaga

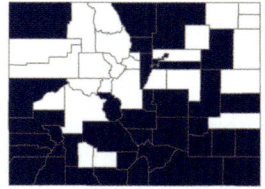

Range & Habitat
A South Asian native, Purslane is now found worldwide. In Colorado, like most of America, it's weed–like in habitat and found in disturbed soils, growing up to 8000' (though it's usually found at lower elevations). Garden plots, vacant lots, and field and trail edges are some standard places to look for Purslane.

As an annual, Purslane responds vigorously to summer rains; it's available for just 1–2 months per year.

Edible Uses
Like most other plants of the Portulaca genus, all parts of Purslane are edible. The young leaves and stems are the best tasting. They are pleasantly sour and succulent in consistency. Purslane is best eaten raw, as cooking diminishes its flavor and substance. Similar to others in the Purslane family, the plant is nutritious. It is high in omega–3 essential fatty acids, calcium, magnesium, potassium and vitamins C and A.

Medicinal Uses
There are no medicinal uses for Purslane.

Cautions & Special Note
Small to moderate amounts of Purslane are fine consumed raw; however, if large amounts are being eaten on a regular basis, I suggest first boiling and rinsing the plant. This removes much of the leaves' oxalate content.

Numerous plants in the Purslane family (Portulacaceae) are edible. Bitterroot (Lewisia), Miner's lettuce and Spring beauty (Claytonia), and Jewels of Opar (Talinum) are a few notable species.

Sustenance Index: Low
Pictured: *Portulaca oleracea*

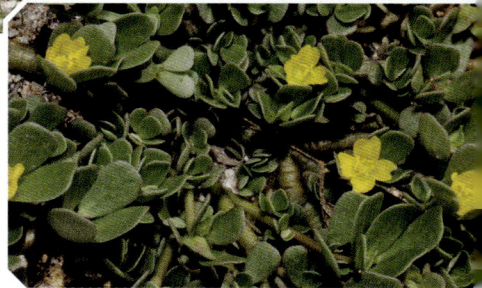

Raspberry
Rubus idaeus ssp. strigosus

Other Common Names
Red raspberry, American red raspberry, Western red raspberry

Range & Habitat
Raspberry is a common Rocky Mountain understory herbaceous shrub. It's found throughout all the higher mountains of Colorado. Associated with Fir, Spruce, and Aspen, look to creek and drainage sides, canyon bottoms, and moist slopes and hills.

Edible Uses
Raspberry fruit found in the wild tends to be a little smaller than store-bought cultivars; however, at peak ripeness they are just as sweet possibly even more so. They are fine consumed fresh and can too be utilized as a preserve or jelly base. In all ways, consider wild Raspberry identical in use to the fruit found in commerce.

Relatively high in vitamin C. the fruit contains approximately 30 milligrams per 8 ounces. It also is a far source of a number of B vitamins and vitamin E.

Medicinal Uses
Raspberry leaf tea is a female reproductive tonic mainly used throughout the last trimester of pregnancy. The tea is also soothing to urinary tract irritations.

Cautions
There are no cautions for Raspberry.

Special Note
Raspberry is closely related to Thimbleberry, Dewberry, Blackberry, and Salmonberry (all Rubus species). American and East Asian Raspberry is Rubus idaeus ssp. strigosus. Store bought Raspberries are from cultivars of European raspberry (Rubus idaeus ssp. idaeus).

Sustenance Index: Medium
Pictured: *Rubus idaeus ssp. strigosus*

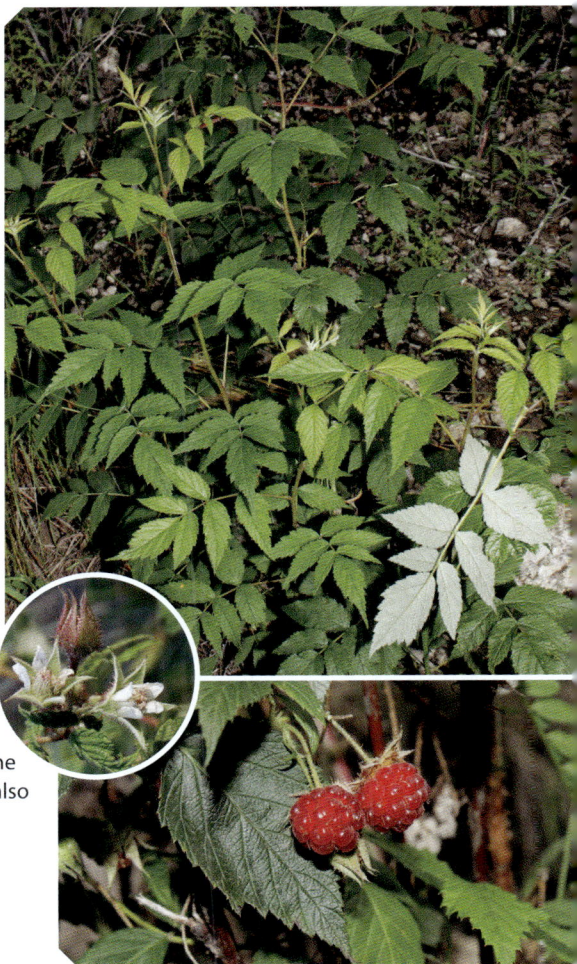

Russian Olive
Elaeagnus angustifolia

Other Common Names
Silver Berry, Oleaster, Wild olive

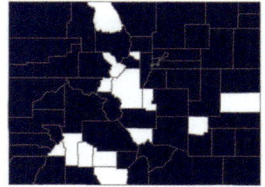

Range & Habitat
Native to Asia, Russian olive is abundantly found as an exotic throughout the inter–mountain western states. It's populous enough in Colorado to be considered invasive. Here it tends to out–compete native trees and shrubs particularly next to waterways (lower to middle elevations).

Edible Uses
I'm not a big fan of Russian olive as a wild edible. It has too high of a tannin content for my taste. However, if you decide to proceed, it's important to allow the fruit to fully ripen on the tree prior to collection. If picked too soon, the fruit is very astringent and essentially inedible. Pay attention to the fruit around early fall/first frost. Gather them just before to dropping to the ground. At this point they can be eaten raw in limited amounts. They'll still be somewhat astringent and mealy, but slightly sweet too. However, in order to consume them in any quantity, they'll need to be water-leached.

Submerge the fruit in water, changing it daily until the fruit are astringency–free. Once relatively free of tannins, a seasoning brine is added. This is similar to traditional raw olive processing.

Once roasted, the seed of Russian olive is edible as well. It's best ground into a meal and added to other flours in baking.

Medicinal Uses, Cautions, & Special Note
The powdered dried fruit mixed with a beverage is a traditional diarrhea remedy. This is due to the berry's abundance of tannins. Relatedly, too much will cause constipation. Russian olive is closely related to Autumn olive, a more edible Wild olive species (Elaeagnus umbellata).

Sustenance Index: Low
Pictured: *Elaeagnus angustifolia*

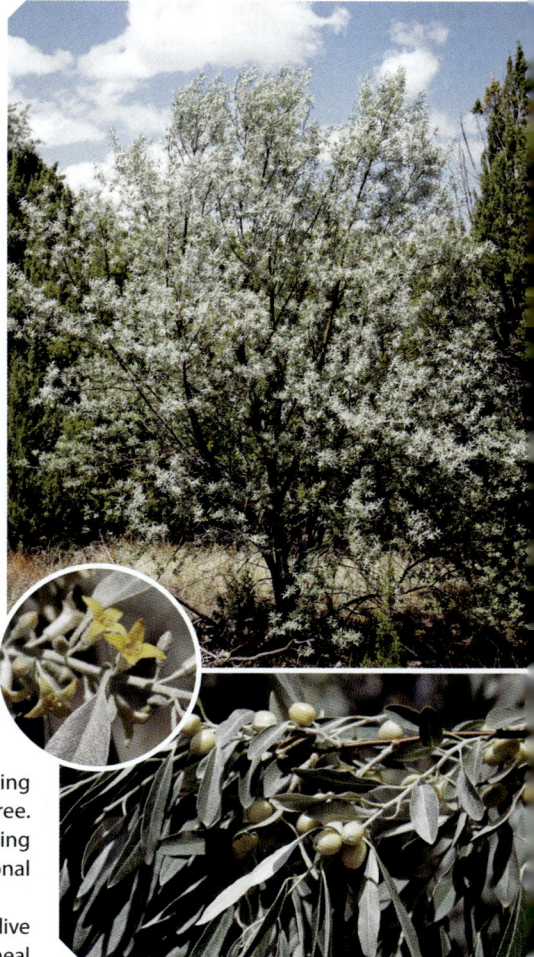

Salsify
Tragopogon dubius, T. porrifolius, T. pratensis

Other Common Names
Yellow salsify, Goat's beard, Oyster root, Purple salsify, Meadow salsify

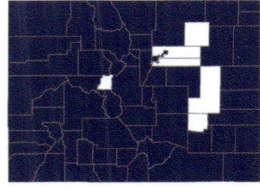

Range & Habitat
All Coloradan Salsify species are non–native and originally from Europe. They do well at high to middle elevations, particularly in grassy areas that have at one time been disturbed – lawn and park edges, trailsides, embankments, etc.

Tragopogon dubius (Yellow salsify) is the most commonly encountered species (yellow flowers). It's found statewide. T. porrifolius (Purple salsify) and T. pratensis (Meadow salsify) (yellow flowers), are not quite as abundant, but nevertheless, found throughout middle–mountain elevations.

Edible Uses
The upper parts (flower, leaf, and stem) are picked and eaten raw, or steamed/sautéed as a cooked green. A good tasting and mild plant, the above–ground parts are non–bitter and very palatable. Try to collect the foliage before the flower goes to seed. It is more tender early in the season.

Salsify roots can be eaten raw, but most find them better if first boiled/steamed/sautéed. They are mildly bitter-tasting (I don't think they taste like oysters) and provide more complex carbohydrates than the upper parts. The roots of older plants tend to be woody, especially if in their second or third year.

Medicinal Uses, Cautions, & Special Note
There are no significant medicinal uses or cautions for Salsify. All parts of the plant exude a milky latex if cut or torn. Another identifying feature is its large softball–sized seed puff-ball.

Sustenance Index: Medium
Pictured: *Tragopogon dubius*

Serviceberry
Amelanchier alnifolia, A. utahensis

Other Common Names
Alder–leaf serviceberry, Utah serviceberry

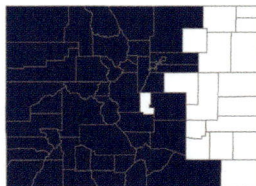

Range & Habitat
Serviceberry is primarily a shrub of the Rocky Mountains (and Pacific–States). Colorado hosts two species: Amelanchier alnifolia (Alder–leaf serviceberry) and A. utahensis (Utah serviceberry).

Absent from the eastern Plains, both species are commonly found throughout the mountains. Of the two, Utah serviceberry grows slightly lower in elevation.

Look for both shrubs on rocky hillsides and slopes, with a stream or drainage not far away. Ponderosa pine, Juniper, and Oak are usual companion trees.

Edible Uses
Ripening mid to late summer, the purple fruit are eaten raw. They are seed–filled, but if found in optimal condition, are still sweet and juicy. If discovered early, late, or environmentally stressed, the fruit is often dry and mealy, and is a better candidate for a jam or jelly preparation.

Medicinal Uses
Aside from the leaves' mild astringency, there are no medicinal uses for Serviceberry.

Cautions
Serviceberry seeds, like most from the Rose family, contain traces of cyanogenic glycosides. Drying/grinding/heating destroys these compounds. Fear not though – if accidentally consumed (small amounts), there is little to be concerned of from Serviceberry seed. There are no cautions for the fleshy portion of the fruit.

Sustenance Index: Medium
Pictured: *Amelanchier alnifolia (top & circle)* | *Amelanchier utahensis (bottom)*

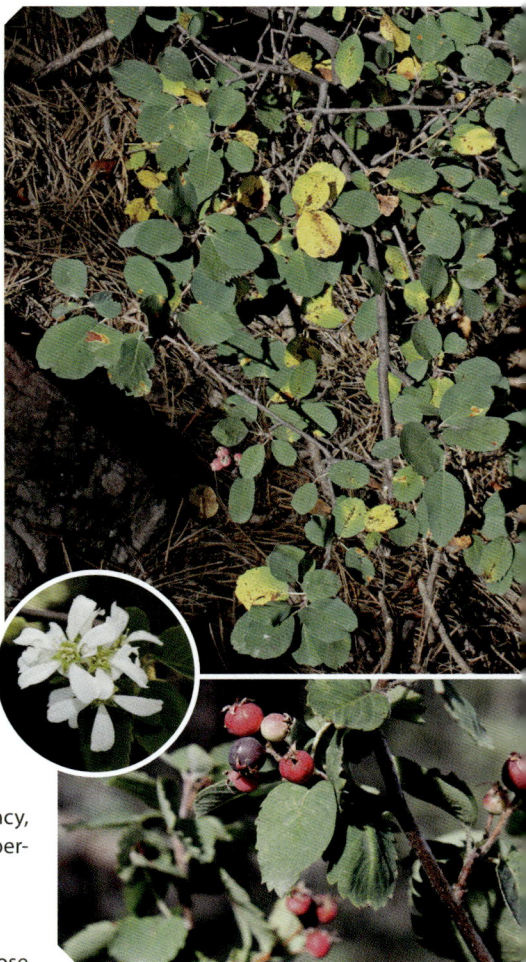

Sheep's Sorrel
Rumex acetosella

Other Common Names
Field sorrel, Red sorrel

Range & Habitat
This non–native herbaceous perennial is somewhat common to higher
elevations throughout Colorado. Pre-
ferring disturbed soils, look for this
small herb in full sun exposures along
trailsides, ditches, and dirt roadsides.

Edible Uses
Sheep's sorrel is best utilized as a
fresh herb in salads or as a garnish.
The leaves being the main edible
part, are tangy and sour-tasting (oxalates). Moderate amounts can be
consumed raw; however, if eating
more than a hand-full, I recommend
first giving the leaves a quick boil and
rinse. This will diminish some of its
oxalate content.

Medicinal Uses
Sheep's sorrel is not particularly medicinal; however, the plant's therapeutic void has not stopped product
hucksters from promoting it as part
of a 'cancer–cure' herbal combination.

Cautions
Excess consumption of oxalates may lead
to urinary tract irritation and stone development (if prone to their formation). Boil-
ing/rinsing Sheep's sorrel reduces its oxalate concentration.

Special Note
Two characteristics will help in identifying Sheep's sorrel: 1) sour taste; 2) the leaves are
arrow–shaped with pointed base lobes (hastate). Although unrelated, Sheep's sorrel and
Sorrel (Oxalis) are identical in edible use (foliage).

Sustenance Index: Low
Pictured: *Rumex acetosella*

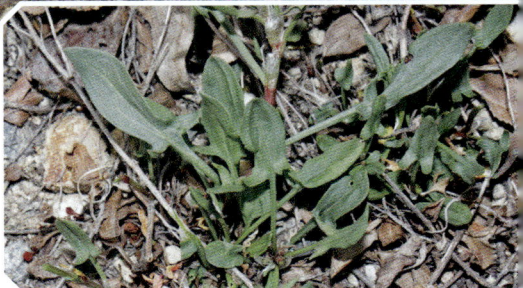

45

Smartweed
Persicaria spp.

Other Common Names
Lady's thumb, Knotweed

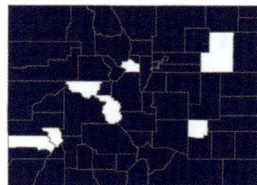

Range & Habitat
Colorado is home to nearly ten species of Persicaria, the majority of which are native. Persicaria maculosa (Spotted lady's thumb) is the most widespread introduced species.

An easily encountered group of plants, nearly all bodies of water in Colorado have at least one species of Smartweed thriving on its banks; look to the sides of perennial rivers, ponds, and lakes.

Edible Uses
Gather the just–emerging young leaves and tender stems, preferably before the plant flowers. In small amounts they can be chopped and eaten fresh as a salad ingredient. Larger quantities are consumed as a boiled green. With a little seasoning, they make a fine–tasting, spinach/chard–like wild vegetable.

Medicinal Uses
Not commonly used today, Smartweed species were employed by various Indian tribes for an array of minor issues. Interestingly, there is some application similarity between Persicaria and Rumex (Yellowdock). Both plants belong to the same family and are chemically affiliated.

Cautions & Special Note
Water contamination and harmful water-borne microorganisms are likely the greatest concern when utilizing Smartweed. Make sure to give the leaves a clean water rinse (or boil) prior to consuming. See Tule for instructions on a sanitizing wash. One feature that helps to identify several Smartweed species is a notable mid–leaf purple spot (like a lady's partial thumb print).

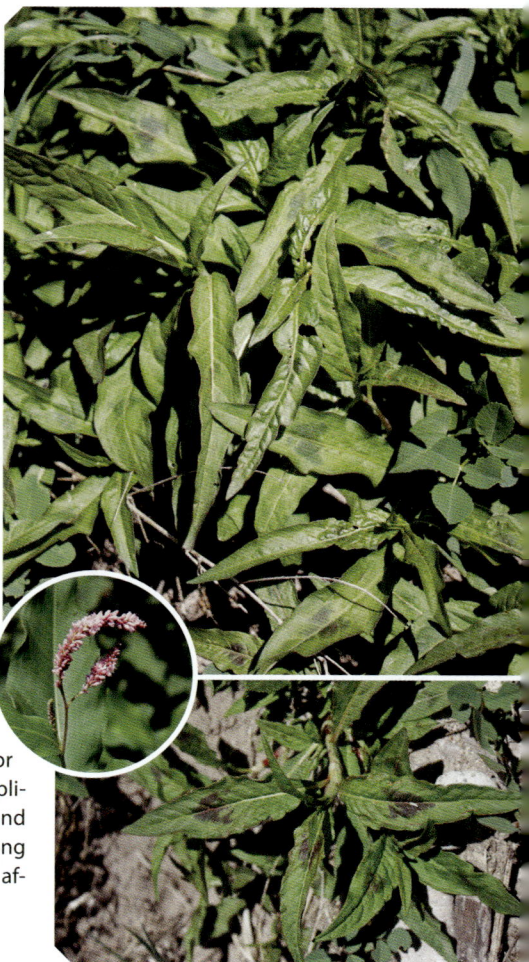

Sustenance Index: Low
Pictured: *Persicaria spp.*

46

Spiderwort
Tradescantia occidentalis

Other Common Names
Prairie spiderwort, Western spiderwort

Range & Habitat
Prairie spiderwort is the only Tradescantia species found in Colorado. It's local to the central–eastern parts of the state on rocky slopes and in grassland areas. It prefers full–sun exposures.

Edible Uses
All parts of Spiderwort are edible, either fresh or cooked. Needing no preparation, the entire above–ground young plant (flower, stem, and leaf) is simply picked when encountered and eaten raw. Some parts may be a little fibrous, but nevertheless, the plant is pleasant tasting.

The roots are slender, but thickened. They are mild and semi–starchy (sometimes a little fibrous). Eat them raw or better yet, chop, simmer, and season as a cooked vegetable. Bland–tasting, they are fine consumed solo or in combination with other edibles.

Medicinal Uses & Cautions
There are no medicinal uses or cautions for Spiderwort.

Special Note
Spiderwort is botanically related to Dayflower (same family – Commelinaceae), another edible plant that grows to the south and east of Colorado. Both plants have identical edible uses and should be considered interchangeable.

The ornamental species of Spiderwort (Wandering Jew – Tradescantia fluminensis and T. zebrina), grown as a ground cover in warmer parts of the country, are also edible. The young fleshy leaves are best chopped and used as a salad ingredient.

Sustenance Index: Medium
Pictured: *Tradescantia occidentalis*

47

Squaw Apple
Peraphyllum ramosissimum

Other Common Names
Wild crab apple

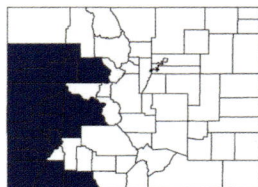

Range & Habitat
Squaw apple has a wide distribution in a number of the western states, however, it's only an occasional shrub and usually not encountered in significant numbers. If more than several plants are found in a single outing, consider yourself lucky. In Colorado, Squaw apple is limited to the foothills of the Western Slope at elevations of 6000'–8000', in association with scrub vegetation, Gambel oak, Pinyon/Juniper, and Ponderosa pine.

Edible Uses
The fruit ripens in middle to late summer. At this point the outer skin will be yellowish–orange in color. The flesh is mildly sweet and certainly not unpleasant. Each fruit contains several hard seeds, which should be discarded. Consume Squaw apple fresh or too the fruit is a good jelly/drying candidate once de–seeded.

When encountered early in the season, the fruit is reddish–green. Like most other Rose family fruits, I'm assuming the flesh will be too astringent/mealy/poor–tasting to eat at this juncture.

Medicinal Uses
Squaw apple is not a significant medicinal plant.

Cautions
The seeds likely contain small amounts of cyanogenic glycosides, like Apple seeds, Cherry pits, etc. They are best disposed of.

Sustenance Index: Medium
Pictured: *Peraphyllum ramosissimum*

Thimbleberry
Rubus parviflorus

Other Common Names
Western thimbleberry

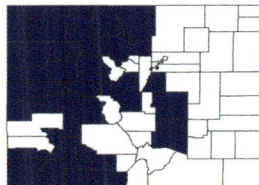

Range & Habitat
Thimbleberry's main territory consti-
tutes the Rocky Mountains and higher mountains of the Pacific states.

In Colorado, it's reliably found
throughout the interior ranges – San
Juans, Park Range, Front Range, etc.
Look for the plant in dappled shade
from Aspen and conifers. It's largely
non–existent in the Plains and non–
forested basins and plateaus.

Edible Uses
Ripening mid to late summer, Thimbleberry's fruit tastes similar to Raspberry, yet not quite as succulent. They
are fine eaten fresh – the drupelets
peeled away from the drupe core.
They too can be dried for future use
or prepared as a jam/jelly.

Thimbleberry is like Raspber-
ry in nutritional aspects. It contains
good amounts of vitamin C, potassium, and magnesium.

Medicinal Uses
Thimbleberry leaf is used as a Raspberry leaf replacement. Drink the tea as urinary tract soother and female reproductive
astringent.

Cautions
There are no cautions for Thimbleberry.

Special Note
Though Blackberry, Raspberry, and Thim-
bleberry are closely related (Rubus genus), Thimbleberry is the only plant of the bunch with
a simple leaf (it is not comprised of multiple leaflets). Blackberry is 5–parted; Raspberry is
3–parted.

Sustenance Index: Medium
Pictured: *Rubus parviflorus*

49

Thistle
Cirsium spp.

Other Common Names
Canada thistle, Bull thistle, Prairie thistle, etc.

Range & Habitat
Sixteen species of thistle are found throughout Colorado, about half of which are widespread. Common to most elevations, one unifying location characteristic for all species is: disturbed soils. Look for Thistle on dirt roadsides, ditches, trailsides, stock–used meadows, and field edges.

Edible Uses
The taproot of first or early second year plants (leaves still a basal rosette) will be found crisp and crunchy with an almost nutty flavor (species variable). As the plant ages (and develops a stalk) the root quickly become fibrous, woody, and inedible. Gathered during the proper time the root is fine raw, but can also be chopped, cooked, and seasoned accordingly.

Thistle stalk also deserve mention as they are too an often overlooked edible. It needs to be immature, just–emerging, and flexible. Cut the stalk from the base of the plant. Remove the leaves and tops (usually spiny) and peel away the outer layer until the inner palatable part is revealed. The stalk core is mild tasting and can be eaten raw, cooked, or even pickled. The larger species of Thistle (Bull thistle for instance) will be best for stalk uses.

Medicinal Uses & Cautions
There are no significant medicinal uses for Thistle. Edible thistles are unrelated in application to Milk thistle (Silybum marianum), a useful herbal medicine for the liver.

A number of Thistle species are listed as noxious weeds. Be sure herbicides have not been used recently prior to collection.

Sustenance Index: Medium
Pictured: *Cirsium parryi (top)* | *C. neomexicanum (circle)* | *Cirsium scariosum (bottom)*

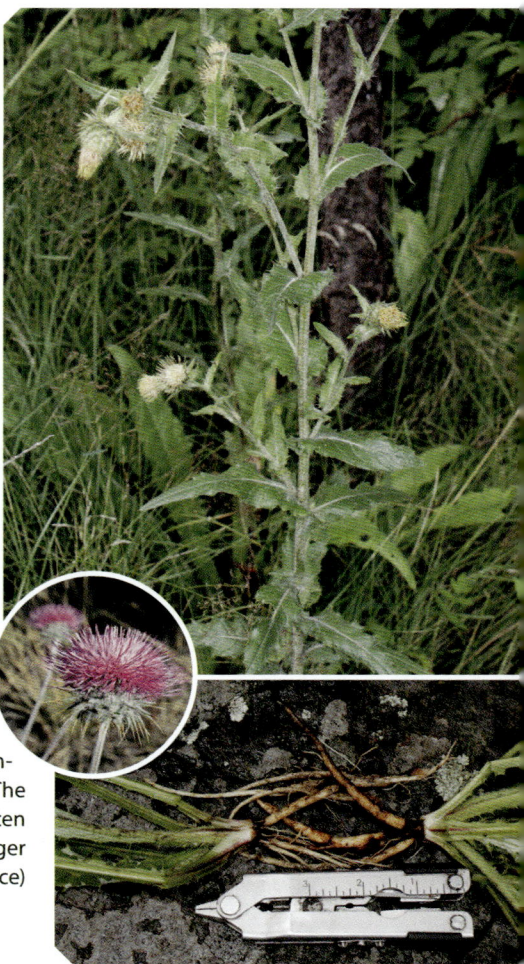

50

Tuber Starwort
Pseudostellaria jamesiana

Other Common Names
Sticky starwort

Range & Habitat
Tuber starwort is a common herbaceous perennial throughout the Middle and Southern Rockies. In Colorado look for it at middle mountain elevations: 7000'–9000'. The plant prefers drier exposures with dappled shade, often in association with conifers, Aspen, and/or Gambel oak. It's absent from desert elevations and the Plains.

Edible Uses
The small tuberous rhizomes are the main food item. They lie not far below the ground's surface, which makes their procurement easy – often hands alone can be used. Once the stringy part of the rhizome is removed the tubers are fine consumed fresh (mild tasting and crunchy). They too can be wrapped in foil and baked like a potato if a warm–starchy meal is desired. Due to the plant's abundance and carbohydrate content, it's an under–appreciated wild food. The foliage too can be eaten...but it's nothing to write home about.

Medicinal Uses & Cautions
There are no significant medicinal uses or cautions for Tuber starwort.

Special Note
When not in flower, at first glance, the above–ground portion of Tuber starwort appears like so many other mountain herbs. However, some key differences that help in identification are as follows: leaves form directly opposite from each other, they are sessile (lack leaf stems) and lance–shaped. Also, each leaf pair is usually offset 30–45 degrees from the previous set. If still in doubt, just dig up a patch – small crunchy tubers connected to thin rhizomes? If so, it's Tuber starwort.

Sustenance Index: Medium
Pictured: *Pseudostellaria jamesiana*

Tule
Schoenoplectus acutus (Scirpus acutus)

Other Common Names
Common tule, Hardstem bulrush

Range & Habitat
Two varieties of Tule are found throughout the state: var. acutus and var. occidentalis. For both plants, appearance (and uses) are practically identical. Marsh, lake, and reservoir margins are common habitats for Tule.

Edible Uses
Tule is like Cattail in regard to edibility; meaning almost all parts can be used. The springtime emerging young stems/shoots are eaten raw or cooked. After the stems have matured, they are cut at the base and peeled of their outer sheathing layers. This exposes each stem base's tender edible core. Tule's rhizomes are edible, though the younger budding ends are the choice part. They need little preparation. The older rhizome should be peeled and cooked first due age–related toughness/sponginess. Indians would also dry these parts and grind them into a flour for later use.

    Both Tule pollen (knock the flowering clusters in a bucket) and seeds (post flowering) are collected and utilized in various ways. Tule pollen is high in protein and can be mixed with other flours in baking or simply mixed with water and eaten as a gruel. Grind the seeds (also high in protein) and eat accordingly.

Medicinal Uses, Cautions, & Special Note
There are no medicinal uses for Tule. If consuming the rhizomes raw, consider a diluted chlorine bleach soak: mix 1 tablespoon of unscented chlorine bleach (regular Clorox) in 1 gallon of potable water. Soak the plant material in the solution for 15 minutes. Rinse and eat. Though root sizes will vary, most other Schoenoplectus species (Bulrush) are edible as well. Mats, baskets, and even primitive garments were once woven from the mature stems.

Sustenance Index: High
Pictured: *Schoenoplectus acutus var. occidentalis*

Tumble Mustard

Sisymbrium altissimum

Other Common Names
Tall mustard, Hedge mustard, Jim Hill mustard, Wild mustard

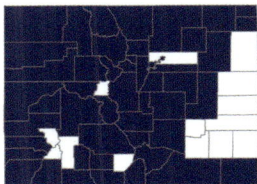

Range & Habitat
Tumble mustard is possibly the most common weed Mustard found in Colorado. Look for it in disturbed soils. Dirt parking lot edges, trailsides, dried cattle tanks, and drainages where some moisture has lingered are some of its usual places.

Edible Uses
The young leaves and tops (flowers and young seed pods) are best eaten as a spicy garnish or salad addition. For the consumption of larger amounts, be sure to steam/sauté these parts first. Heat dissipates much of the plant's Mustard oils, enabling greater quantities to be eaten.

Tumble mustard is a little more coarse and hairy than Wintercress. However, once cooked, differences between the two plants are minimal.

Medicinal Uses & Cautions
Like all Mustard species, Tumble mustard contains ample amounts of glucosinolates (Mustard oil). Responsible for the plant's spicy taste, this constituent group tends to be relieving to ingestion (small handful of the fresh plant), and for women, stimulating to menses (larger amounts). Too much of the fresh plant will irritate the gastrointestinal tract and occasionally the kidneys.

Special Note
For the dedicated, the small seeds can be used as a Mustard seed replacement; however, they are very tiny and may not be worth the effort.

Sustenance Index: Low
Pictured: *Sisymbrium altissimum*

53

Watercress
Nasturtium officinale (Rorippa nasturtium–aquaticum)

Other Common Names
Creek mustard, Berro

Range & Habitat
Common throughout most of North America, look for this naturalized semi–aquatic perennial along gently flowing streams and springs. Watercress tops–out in elevation at about 8000'. It is usually found in low to middle elevation habitats.

Edible Uses
Like other mustards, Watercress makes a nice addition to foraged salads and mixed greens. It is warming and spicy, and as an accent, is pleasantly stimulating to the palate. Most people find a mouth full of fresh Watercress too spicy; however, larger quantities can be eaten if first boiled or steamed.

Medicinal Uses
A small handful is useful for stomach bloating and indigestion.

Cautions
Large amounts of fresh Watercress can irritate the kidneys, and in some women, stimulate menses.

Special Note
Watercress is one of the better tasting mustards. It has a well–deserved reputation as a leafy edible. Unlike true Mustard (Brassica or Sinapis), which is best known as the seed (and Mustard greens) source for the condiment, Watercress has a longer picking/eating season due to the extra hydration provided by its water environs.

Before collecting any water–thriving plant, be aware of the water's quality. Agricultural/industrial runoff, cattle activity, and so on, can adversely affect the water and local plant life. If microorganisms are suspected, a diluted chlorine bleach soak then rinse is wise. *See Tule.*

Sustenance Index: Low
Pictured: *Nasturtium officinale*

Wild Onion
Allium spp.

Other Common Names
Tapertip onion, Nodding onion, Geyer's onion, Large–flowering onion, Textile onion

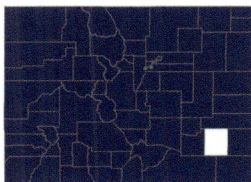

Range & Habitat
Colorado is home to ten onion species. Allium acuminatum (Tapertip onion), A. cernuum (Nodding onion), A. geyeri (Geyer's onion), A. macropetalum (Large–flowering onion), and A. textile (Textile onion) are a number of the more abundant. They populate a variety of habitats – from high desert, grassland/Prairie, to Ponderosa pine forests and meadows.

Edible Uses
The entire plant – leaf, stalk (scape), flowers, and bulb are equally edible. The bulb usually has the strongest flavor; the herbaceous portions – the mildest. All parts can be eaten fresh (limited); however, for the consumption of larger amounts (bulb), it should first be cooked/baked. This will remove much of the bulb's harshness. Wrapped in foil with a bouillon cube and then set on campfire coals for 10–15 minutes is a fine way to proceed.

Medicinal Uses, Cautions, & Special Note
In terms of medicinal strength, Wild onion can be thought of as a diminutive Garlic (another Allium). A Wild onion honey steep makes a serviceable cold and flu application. It will be found mildly antibacterial and antiviral. Too much raw Wild onion will cause digestive upset.

All Wild onion species are distinguishable from other monocots by their distinctive onion scent. In other words, if it looks like a Wild onion, yet has no onion smell, unless properly identified as another edible plant, then do not eat it. It is not Wild onion, but likely another related plant – some of which are edible, but some too are toxic (for instance, Deathcamas).

Sustenance Index: Medium
Pictured: *Allium cernuum (top)* | *Allium macropetalum (circle)* | *Allium acuminatum (bottom)*

55

Wild Rose
Rosa acicularis, R. arkansana, R. nutkana, R. woodsii

Other Common Names
Prickly rose, Prairie rose, Nootka rose, Woods' rose

Range & Habitat
Except for desert elevations, Wild rose is common in Colorado. Three species are found throughout parts or all the state's sub–chains, at middle–high to high elevations (in association with conifers/Aspen). Of the group, Wood's rose is the most abundant. Rosa arkansana (Prairie rose) is found in the foothills of the Front Range and Sangre de Cristos, then east across the Prairie. All species prefer slopes and drainage sides, either in partial or full sun exposures.

Edible Uses
The fruit of Wild rose (any Rose species) is called a 'hip'. Ripening late summer to early fall, they can be eaten fresh, but they are not the best tasting: seed–filled/insipid. Their best preparation will be as a jelly or syrup base. Wild rose hips' high vitamin content makes it an important forage if nutritional deficiency (especially vitamin C) is suspected. For this reason, the dried hips were an important cold–season food supplement, especially if the diet was limited (cabin shut–in: canned food/jerky/beans/etc.). Relatedly, crushed hips were a common pemmican ingredient.

Medicinal Uses, Cautions, & Special Note
The encapsulated hip powder (or simply mixed with water), taken internally, is a well–known nutritional supplement (especially vitamin C, minerals, and health–promoting lipids). The hip powder is also broadly antiinflammatory and tissue/skin supportive. The leaves are mildly astringent and used as a poultice on minor bites, stings, and burns. Wild rose is caution–free. Cultivated Roses are used the same way as Wild rose.

Sustenance Index: Medium
Pictured: *Rosa woodsii*

56

Wild Strawberry
Fragaria vesca, F. virginiana

Other Common Names
Woodland strawberry, Virginia strawberry

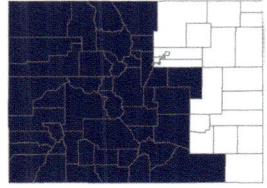

Range & Habitat
Range and habitat (and physical characteristics) for both species are essentially interchangeable, with Virginia strawberry being the more populous of the two.

    Common throughout all of Colorado's higher elevations, Wild strawberry is most often found in dappled shade with Fir, Spruce, and/or Aspen.

Edible Uses
The edibility of Wild strawberry needs little explanation; it is just as tasty as garden–grown or store–bought Strawberry (usually the cultivar – Fragaria X ananassa).

    Eat the fruit fresh, dehydrated for later, or prepared as a jam/jelly or preserve. Like the cultivated type, Wild strawberry is high in potassium and contains fair amounts of vitamin C. The drawbacks to Wild strawberry are its small fruit size and erratic fruit development. Plants lower in elevation and/or at lower latitudes are often sterile.

Medicinal Uses
Wild strawberry leaf is mildly astringent. As a topically applied poultice, it is arresting and inflammation–reducing to minor cuts and scrapes. Internally, the leaf tea is used as a substitute for Raspberry leaf tea (female reproductive tonic).

Cautions & Special Note
There are no cautions for Wild strawberry. It belongs to the Rose family and is related to Blackberry, Raspberry, Wild rose, and Thimbleberry.

Sustenance Index: Medium
Pictured: *Fragaria virginiana*

Wild Sunflower
Helianthus annuus

Other Common Names
Western sunflower, Common sunflower, etc.

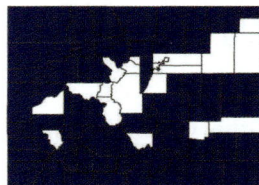

Range & Habitat
Wild sunflower is common throughout much of Colorado (and America too). Habitats above desert elevations but below the higher mountains are good places to look for the plant: roadsides, trailsides, forest openings, meadows, pastures, and floodplains.

Edible Uses
Clip the seed heads from the upper stems when they are almost fully mature and dry. After drying in a paper bag or box, garble the seeds from the seed head. Eat as is (thin hull and all) or grind/sift and utilize the seeds as a meal. High in protein and essential oils, they are very nutritious.

The young flower buds are snipped from the stems and simmered for 10–15 minutes. Rinsed and seasoned, they make a fair cooked vegetable.

Medicinal Uses
There are no medicinal uses for Wild sunflower.

Cautions
There are no cautions for Wild sunflower.

Special Note
Wild species are also a favorite of birds – if you wait until the seed heads are completely dry on the plant before collecting, they will be eaten.

Garden varieties of Sunflower are cultivars. They have been selected and bred over the years to produce the sunflower seed of commerce.

Jerusalem artichoke is also a Sunflower (*Helianthus tuberosus*) of sorts. But unlike Wild sunflower, Jerusalem artichoke is cultivated for its edible tuberous root.

Sustenance Index: High
Pictured: *Helianthus annuus*

Wintercress
Barbarea vulgaris, B. orthoceras

Other Common Names
Yellow rocket, American wintercress, Erectpod wintercress

Range & Habitat
Two Wintercress species are found in Colorado – non–native Barbarea vulgaris, and native B. orthoceras. The non–native species is a bit more common than the other. They are similar in appearance and found at elevations of 5500'–9500', almost always in moist/lower–lying soils.

Edible Uses
Like others in the Mustard family, Wintercress has a pronounced spicy–pungent–mustard taste. The young leaves, flowers, and immature seed pods are consumed fresh, in small amounts, as a salad accent or garnish. Boiled or sautéed briefly, greater quantities can be eaten without the occasional irritating qualities of the fresh plant – heat dissipates most of the plant's mustard oils.

Medicinal Uses
Eat a small handful of the fresh leaf if suffering from indigestion (not heartburn). Many find its stimulating nature relieving to gastric stasis and bloating.

Cautions & Special Note
For women, too much of the fresh plant may stimulant menses. Additionally, I've observed large amounts of the fresh plant cause kidney sensitivity and stomach unease. The causative principles for this are known as glucosinolates, a group of volatiles common to most Mustard family plants. Small amounts of these compounds are fine; large amounts are irritating. Another mountain/moist–soil growing Mustard found at similar elevations is Bog yellowcress (Rorippa palustris). It too is herbaceous with yellow flowers and elongated seedpods. In terms of edibility, it can be treated the same as Wintercress.

Sustenance Index: Low
Pictured: *Barbarea vulgaris*

Yellowdock
Rumex crispus

Other Common Names
Curly dock, Narrowleaf dock

Range & Habitat
Found throughout middle elevations, Yellowdock is common state–wide. It's almost always encountered in moist–disturbed soils. Lake, pond, and stream sides, cattle tanks, and other areas where the ground remains hydrated are good places to look for Yellowdock.

Edible Uses
Yellowdock makes for a fair green. The younger leaves and flexible stems are palatable raw (similar to the texture of kale or chard); however, they're better if first sautéed or steamed. Some plants will be more sour/tart than others – this is mainly due to calcium oxalate content within the leaf/stem.

Medicinal Uses
Yellowdock is considered the most important medicinal species of the genus. It's a root medicine and its therapeutic effects have influence over the liver, intestines, and skin.

Cautions
There are only minor cautions for the consumption of Yellowdock greens. For some people, the oxalate content may be irritating to the kidneys, but this is only a problem if consumed raw in large quantities.

Special Note
Rumex hymenosepalus (Wild rhubarb) is another edible (young stalks) Rumex species; however, it is found at lower desert elevations in the western part of the state. Yellowdock is native to Eurasia. Now though, it grows worldwide, and in many areas is considered invasive. It is likely one of the oldest non–native plants found in North America. 'Crispus' refers to the leaves' crinkled edges.

Sustenance Index: Low
Pictured: *Rumex crispus*

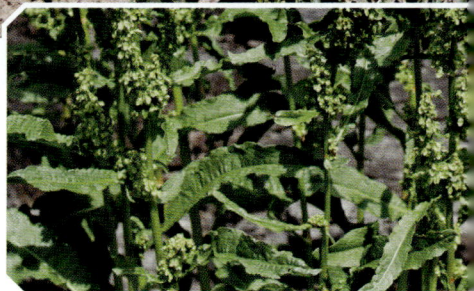

Yucca
Yucca glauca

Other Common Names
Soapweed yucca, Great Plains yucca, Prairie yucca

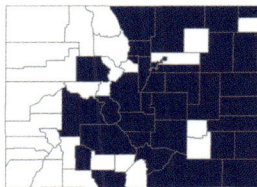

Range & Habitat
Yucca glauca has the most expansive range of all Yucca species in America. From Texas it is found throughout the Great Plains to Canada. In Colorado, it mainly inhabits the Plains of the eastern part of the state. Here it is common and abundant.

Edible Uses
The immature stalk of Yucca glauca (and all other Yucca species for that matter) is harvested for food. Yucca's palatability has everything to do with collection timing. Clip the last foot or so of the immature and flexible stalk as soon as it begins to arise in the spring (pre–flower). If it is even slightly woody the 1–2 week edibility window has been missed. Regardless of timing, further along towards the base it becomes more fibrous, bitter, and soapy (inedible). Strip away the flower buds and outer skin, exposing the inner core. Eat the pealed stalk raw (limited), or better yet, boil, rinse, and season the material as a wild vegetable. This process also helps to remove any saponin–related bitterness that is common to Yucca.

Medicinal Uses, Cautions, & Special Note
Yucca root is an herbal treatment for arthritis. The commonest preparation is the dried and powdered encapsulated root. Be aware of possible stomach upset with the ingestion of excess raw material.

Yucca's leaf fibers are utilized as cordage. Unlike Banana yucca (Yucca baccata), the fruit of woody–capsule types (Y. glauca) are inedible. A weak soap solution is made from the roots.

Sustenance Index: Medium
Pictured: *Yucca glauca*

61

Index

A

Acer negundo 8
Achnatherum hymenoides
24
acorns 18
Alder–leaf serviceberry 44
Allium acuminatum 55
  cernuum 55
  geyeri 55
  macropetalum 55
  textile 55
Alpine false springparsley
31
Amaranth 4, 25, 34
Amaranthus 4
Amelanchier alnifolia 44
  utahensis 44
American red raspberry 41
  wintercress 59
anthocyanins 5
Anticlea 3
antioxidant 5, 7, 15
Apache 6
Arizona 12, 13
Ash leaf maple 8
Asparagus 5, 9, 32
  officinalis 5
Astragalus 3
Atriplex dioica 34
  hortensis 34
  micrantha 34
  patula 34
  rosea 34
Autumn olive 42

B

Banana yucca 61
Barbarea orthoceras 59
  vulgaris 59
Barberry 14
Beeplant 6
Bee spiderflower 6
Berberis aquifolium var.
    repens 14
  repens 14
Berro 54
Bilberry 7
Bitterroot 40
Blackberry 41, 49, 57
Black currant 15
  gooseberry 19
Blueberry 7
Box elder 8
Bracken fern 9

Brassica 54
Broadleaf cattail 11
Brown–spined prickly pear
39
Bull thistle 50
Buttercup family 29

C

California 12, 28, 33
  nettle 33
Callirhoe involucrata 12
Calochortus aureus 28
  flexuosus 28
  gunnisonii 28
  nuttallii 28
Caltha leptosepala 29
Canada thistle 50
capers 6, 29
Cardamine cordifolia 23
Carelessweed 4
Cattail 11, 52
Checkermallow 12, 27
Cheeseplant 27
Cheeseweed 27
Chenopodium album 25
  ambrosioides 25
  berlandieri 25
  fremontii 25
Chokecherry 13
Chrysanthemum cinerariae-
    folium 35
Cicuta 3
Cirsium parryi 50
  neomexicanum 50
  scariosum 50
Clammyweed 6
Claytonia 40
Cleomaceae 6
Cleome serrulata 6
Common asparagus 5
  barberry 14
  mallow 27
  monkey flower 30
  sunflower 58
  tule 52
Conium 3
cordage 61
Cota 20
Cottonwood 8
Crataegus erythropoda 22
  rivularis 22
Creek mustard 54
Creeping hollygrape 14
  mahonia 14
Cucurbita foetidissima 10
Curly dock 60
Currant 8, 15, 19
Cymopterus lemmonii 31

D

Dalmatian daisy 35
Dayflower 47
Deathcamas 3, 55
Dewberry 41
Disporum trachycarpum 17
Douglas fir 7, 14
Dwarf bilberry 7

E

Eastern chokecherry 13
Elaeagnus angustifolia 42
  umbellata 42
Elder 8
Elkslip 29
Epazote 25
Erectpod wintercress 59
Erythranthe guttata 30
Espadilla 11
European Black currant 15
Evening primrose 16

F

Fairybells 17
False hellebore 3
  Solomon's Seal 17
Fendler's barberry 14
Fiddleneck 9
Field daisy 35
  sorrel 45
Fir 7, 8, 12, 14, 41, 57
Fragaria vesca 57
  virginiana 57
Fraxinus 8
Fremont's mahonia 14
Front Range 49, 56

G

Gambel oak 7, 18, 48, 51
Garden asparagus 5
  orach 34
Geyer's onion 55
glucosinolates 6, 23
Goat's beard 43
Golden currant 15
Gooseberry 15, 19
Goosefoot 25
Gordolobo 32
Great ox–eye 35
  Plains 12, 61
Greenthread 20
Ground cherry 21
Grouse whortleberry 7
Gunnison's mariposa lily 28

H

Halberdleaf orach 34
Hawthorn 22
Heartleaf bittercress 23
Hedge mustard 53
Helianthus annuus 58
    tuberosus 58
Hollygrape 14
Hooker's evening primrose
    16
Hopi 20
    tea 20
Horse nettle 3
Huckleberry 7
Husk tomato 21

J

Jerusalem artichoke 58
Jewels of Opar 40
Jim Hill mustard 53
Juniper 8, 24, 37, 44, 48

L

lactones 29
Lady's thumb 46
Lambsquarters 25, 34
Lanté 38
Large flowering onion 55
    mountain bittercress 23
Lathyrus 3
Lemonade berry 8, 26
Leucanthemum vulgare 35
Lewisia 40
Little hogweed 40
    mallow 27
    oregongrape 14
Locoweed 3
Longleaf ground cherry 21

M

magnesium 7, 40, 49
Mahonia repens 14
Maianthemum racemosum
    17
    stellatum 17
Mallow 1, 12, 27
    family 12
Malva neglecta 27
    parviflora 27
Maple 8
Mariposa lily 28
Marshmallow root 12
Marsh marigold 29
Maudlin daisy 35
Meadow salsify 43

Milk thistle 50
Mimulus glabratus 30
    guttatus 30
Miner's lettuce 40
Missouri gourd 10
Monkey flower 30
Mountain parsley 31
Mullein 32
Mustard 6, 23, 53, 54, 59
    family 23, 59

N

Narrowleaf cattail 11
    dock 60
Nasturtium officinale 54
Navajo 6, 20, 34
    tea 20
Nettle 33
Nevada 12
New Mexico 13
    pinyon 37
Nodding onion 55
Nootka rose 56

O

Oenothera biennis 16
    elata ssp. hirsutissima 16
    hookeri 16
Oleaster 42
Opuntia macrorhiza 39
    engelmannii 39
    phaeacantha 39
Orach 34
Oregon 12
Oregongrape 14
Oryzopsis hymenoides 24
oxalates 4, 25, 34, 39, 40,
    45, 60
Oxalis 45
Ox-eye daisy 35
Oyster root 43

P

Pacific Northwest 7
Pampa tea 20
Panicgrass 36
Panicum capillare 36
Peavine 3
Peraphyllum ramosissimum
    48
Peritoma serrulata 6
Persicaria 46
Physalis 21
Pine 7, 37
Pinus cembroides var.
    edulis 37

    edulis 37
Pinyon 8, 24, 37, 48
Plantago major 38
    ovata 38
Plantain 38
Poison hemlock 3, 31
    ivy 26
    sumac 26
Polanisia dodecandra 6
Portulaca oleracea 40
potassium 7, 40, 49, 57
Powell's amaranth 4
Prairie rose 56
    spiderwort 47
    thistle 50
    yucca 61
Prickly pear 39
    rose 56
Prosartes trachycarpa 17
Prostrate pigweed 4
Prunus serotina 13
    virginiana var. demissa 13
        var. melanocarpa 13
Pseudocymopterus monta-
        nus 31
Pseudostellaria jamesiana
        51
Pteridium aquilinum 9
Pueblo 6
Punks 11
Purple salsify 43
Purslane 40
    family 40

Q

Quelites 4, 25
Quercus gambelii 18

R

Raspberry 22, 41, 49, 57
Red sorrel 45
Rhus aromatica 26
    glabra 26
Ribes aureum 15
    cereum 15
    inerme 19
    lacustre 19
    laxiflorum 15
    leptanthum 19
    montigenum 15, 19
    nigrum 15
    wolfii 15
River hawthorn 22
Rocky Mountain beeplant
    6
    Checkerbloom 12
    white oak 18

63

Rocky Mountains 6, 12, 14, 15, 18, 23, 31, 41, 44, 49
Rorippa nasturtium–aquaticum 54
palustris 59
Rosa acicularis 56
arkansana 56
nutkana 56
woodsii 56
Rose family 13, 44, 48, 57
hips 22, 56
Rough–fruited fairy–bells 17
mandarin 17
Roundleaf monkey flower 30
Rubus idaeus 41
parviflorus 49
Rumex acetosella 45
crispus 60
hymenosepalus 60
Russian olive 42
orach 34

S

Salmonberry 41
Salsify 43
Saltbush 34
samaras 8
Sambucus 8
Sand amaranth 4
Sangre de Cristos 29, 56
San Juans 29, 49
saponins 10
Schoenoplectus acutus 52
Scirpus acutus 52
Seep monkey flowe 30
Sego lily 28
Serviceberry 22, 44
Sheep's sorrel 45
Sidalcea candida 12
neomexicana 12
Silky mountain rice 24
Silver Berry 42
Silybum marianum 50
Sinapis 54
Sisymbrium altissimum 53
Skunkbush 26
Smartweed 46
soap 10, 61
Soapweed yucca 61
solanine 21
Solanum 3, 21
Sorrel 45
Southern cattail 11
Spear orach 34
Spiderwort 47

Spotted lady's thumb 46
Spring beauty 40
Spruce 7, 8, 12, 14, 41, 57
Squaw apple 48
Squawbush 26
Star Solomon's Seal 17
Sticky starwort 51
Stinging nettle 33
Stinking gourd 10
Stipa hymenoides 24

T

Talinum 40
Tall mustard 53
tannins 18, 42
Tapertip onion 55
Texas 13
Textile onion 55
Thelesperma filifolium 20
megapotamicum 20
subnudum 20
Thimbleberry 41, 49, 57
Thistle 50
Three–leaved sumac 26
Ticklegrass 36
Tomatillo 21
Tradescantia fluminensis 47
occidentalis 47
zebrina 47
Tragopogon dubius 43
porrifolius 43
pratensis 43
Trailing black currant 15
Trumpet gooseberry 19
Tuber starwort 51
Tule 11, 46, 52, 54
Tumble mustard 53
panic 36
Tumbleweed 4
amaranth 4
Tumbling orach 34
Twist–spine prickly pea 39
Two–needle pinyon 37
Typha domingensis 11
latifolia 11

U

Urtica dioica ssp. gracilis 33
gracilenta 33
Utah 12, 44

V

Vaccinium caespitosum 7
corymbosum 7
myrtillus 7
scoparium 7

Veratrum 3
Verbascum thapsus 32
Verdolaga 40
Virginia strawberry 57
vitamin A 7, 25, 40
B 7, 22, 41
C 7, 15, 19, 22, 26, 37, 40, 41, 49, 56, 57
E 41

W

Wandering Jew 47
Watercress 23, 30, 54
Water hemlock 3, 31
Wax currant 15
Western bracken fern 9
chokecherry 13
evening primrose 16
prickly pear 39
red raspberry 41
spiderwort 47
sunflower 58
thimbleberry 49
White checkerbloom 12
marsh marigold 29
oak 18
Whitestem gooseberry 19
Whortleberry 7
Wild asparagus 5
cherry 13
crab apple 48
gourd 10
mustard 53
olive 42
onion 55
rhubarb 60
strawberry 57
sunflower 58
Winecup 12
Wintercress 6, 23, 53, 59
Witchgrass 36
Wolf currant 15
Woodland strawberry 57
Woods' rose 56
Woolly mullein 32
Wyoming 37

Y

Yellowdock 46, 60
Yellow monkey flower 30
rocket 59
salsify 43
Yucca 61
baccata 61
glauca 61